Heave a Bit, Driver

Seven Miles of Laughter

Tony Sanders
& Lorraine Sanders, BA (Hons)

authorHOUSE®

AuthorHouse™ UK Ltd.
500 Avebury Boulevard
Central Milton Keynes, MK9 2BE
www.authorhouse.co.uk
Phone: 08001974150

First published by AuthorHouse 2/3/2009

ISBN: 978-1-4389-3376-4 (sc)

Printed in the United States of America
Bloomington, Indiana

This book is printed on acid-free paper.

Full many a flower is born to blush unseen,
and waste its sweetness on the desert air.
Thomas Gray

Dedication

With love to our family for the help, support,
and enthusiasm they've shown.

Acknowledgements

Tony Sanders had been working at the docks for about three weeks when he met Bob O'Hanlon. They were standing next to each other in the pen when Bob said, "Like cattle, aren't we?" Tony replied, "My thoughts too." The men were lined up like cattle waiting to be hired. When they found out that they both played drums in a rock and roll band they became firm friends, a friendship that continues to this day. Thus special thanks go to Bob for his observations and information.

Thanks also go to ex-dockers from the 'Mayflower' in Bootle.

Contents

Chapter 11
Wokky's Tall Stories **165**

Preface

The stream of ragged men walked down Sandhills from Commercial Road towards the docks in the distance. In twos or threes or singly, they walked to work on the ships lying in the Brocklebank and surrounding docks. They walked with a purposeful gait, conscious of the time it was and knowing they would get there in time to book on and work all day for a pittance, finishing at nine o'clock at night, if they were lucky to get the overtime. If anything should happen, whatever the excuse, they wouldn't be 'on' and another man would be in their place when they got there. Too many men and not enough work gave the employers incredible power, and they wielded it with the help of dockers they picked to be hatch bosses - as it was once described, 'The most brutal of their own kind'.

'Billy' was eighteen, from a staunch Catholic family from Rockingham Street near to the top of Sandhills. He didn't have as far to walk as some of the other men, so he left the house at half past seven. He walked across the canal bridge at the top and followed the road down towards the dock road in the distance. As he neared the junction with Derby Road, he saw some sort of commotion. There seemed to be something blocking the pavement, and men were spilling off it and walking 'round whatever it was. As he got nearer, he caught a glimpse of someone lying on the ground and pushed in to see properly. An elderly man, a docker, well into his fifties, had collapsed, and a couple of men were peering over him not sure what to do. A voice next to him said, 'Heart attack. His lips are blue'. Billy knelt down and cradled the man's head in his arms off the cold pavement flags. The men who'd first stopped realised that somebody else had taken on the mantle of responsibility and they could now walk away, which they did. Others now stepped over him and the man who had collapsed, glancing quickly and just as quickly looking away. Nobody wanted to be late for work. You might never get another job at that yard if you let them down. Dozens and dozens of men stepped over the pair and nobody would help.

Billy heard the man's breath stop and watched as he started to turn a shade of grey. Billy knew that he was dead. He'd never seen anyone die before, but he knew. He knew that the crushing poverty, the slum housing, and the degradation it caused had turned otherwise decent men into frightened sheep. He turned his head up to the sky and shouted out, 'My God, what have they done to us?' He was eighteen; this was Liverpool, the start of the hungry thirties.

Apart from spending six years fighting for his country during the Second World War, Billy had spent his working life at the Liverpool docks, from 1930 until he took severance pay in the early 1970s.

With the dawn of the seventies, things were changing at a rapid rate. Containerisation was coming in, and the docks were top heavy with labour. Employers could soon recoup their investment in new machinery and ships could be turned around and be 'back on the water' in no time – days instead of weeks. A note had been posted in the pen; everybody expected it. It had been talked about for a while. Men were standing in groups after having read it. The note said that anybody who wished to leave the docks would be paid severance pay and that they should report to number two pen for the forms.

Billy the holdsman was well respected in Box One and by everyone who knew him. This was the Billy dockers were looking towards for a lead as they gathered around. "What are you goin' to do, Bill?" someone asked. He pursed his lips thoughtfully as the gang went quiet. "Well ... I've worked down here for thirty-eight years. I've raised children I didn't know. I've put furniture into a house I didn't live in, and all because of the long, long hours spent here. I was always workin'. I'm takin' the money." He turned and walked away from the pen in the direction of box two to fill the forms in. Fourteen other dockers went with him. His name was William James Sanders, the father of Tony Sanders and grandfather of Lorraine Sanders.

Recollections

Tony Sanders started working on the docks in July 1960, a couple of days after his eighteenth birthday. Soon after, the age for working on the docks went up to twenty-one. Men who started work on the docks were required to have polio jabs; Tony needed his mother's signature because he wasn't twenty-one.

Dockers were given a number, which they kept and used whilst working on the docks. This would be given to the timekeeper when being hired for a ship or collecting wages from the clearing house, or for any other purpose that required it. Tony was given the number: 10866.

On his first morning, Tony walked into the pen where they were hiring men. He just shaped up with all the others and didn't know where he was going. A man came along and touched him on the shoulder. Tony asked, "Where's the job?" The man said, "Helenus. The Colony Berth."

The ship had been discharged but there was a small amount of cargo left in it. So, rather than keep the ship and pay the berthing fee for an extra day, they moved her round to the Colony Berth. Tony, along with the other dockers, arrived at the quay before they'd actually hired all the holdsmen. They were told, 'Go on, lads. Go down number three hatch, an' just make a couple of slings up, an' just clear the last bit of cargo'. At the hatch, the boss said, "Ere y' are, lads. Get down below." Tony remembers cocking his leg over the little steel wall that went around the hatch of the ship and looking over the top, thinking, 'Bloody hell. I didn't know ships were so big'. He'd never been that high in his life before. He said, 'It felt like climbing over the edge of the Liver Building'. He looked down and could see a couple of men climbing down the steel ladder, so he just followed them and went all the way down past the deck hold, the 'tween decks, and right to the skin of the ship in the lower hold.

Ships smelt of their cargo. Most ships that were loading would smell of the clean cut wood of the packing cases, diesel oil, and on the Yankee boats the fabulous smell of fresh coffee wafting through the working alley way – a heady mixture that screamed out of ships and the sea.

Tony recalls that misleading information could be seen and heard on radio and television but could be laid to rest by just looking at what was going on at the docks. As in the case of a politician on TV, who said, regarding some conflagration in the Middle East, that 'Her Majesty's government have no intention of being involved in this war'. The same day, army lorries that had been sprayed desert yellow were seen being loaded into a ship on the west side with tons of other military equipment, including armoured cars. So much for truth!

He also remembers that a cross section of opinions could always be heard on the docks and that it was a great education to listen to and to see as young men. Tony states: 'We knew that a big world lay out beyond the line of docks and that we were only passing through'.

Tony remarked that dockers could be extremely kind and thoughtful. The normal practice on a loading boat was for one man's number to be taken from the gang of holdsmen down below, and he would be designated as the Stevedore. This was usually given to an experienced docker, as loading a ship was a serious business. When the timekeeper shouted down for the number of the man picked for the extra shilling a day, there would be a quick roll call among them as to who had the most kids and his number would be shouted up regardless of who was actually doing the stevedoring. It was normally given to a young man with kids on the floor, and this from men whose wages were at the bottom of the industrial scale.

Compassion, too, was evident. A holdsman from box one went to see the priest in St Alphonsus Church and asked him, 'Father, there's a young fella facin' a month in jail if he doesn't pay a twenty-pound fine. Can ye lend me the money?' The priest told him, 'No, I won't lend you the money. I'll give you the money'. The fine was paid and the threat lifted. Six weeks later, the holdsman went to see the priest again and said, 'Father, ye remember the twenty pounds ye gave me to keep a young fella out of jail? Well, I'm now givin' it back to ye'. He handed over four five-pound notes saved from his own wages. It was a considerable sum of money at the time, and was hard earned. Many men who had very little did good deeds.

Introduction

This book was created by the people who worked on the Liverpool docks during the early 1960s. The authors wrote it all down, but thousands of people were responsible for its creation without even knowing. How often has it been said, 'Somebody should write a book about this'?

The book is packed full of funny stories and humorous incidents, many of which are from co-author Tony's own personal experience as a young docker. The stories are all based on actual events.

The stories and humorous tales cover mostly a small area of the Liverpool docks, mainly around the north end, although the humour was apparent along the whole line of docks. However, some tragic events have been included in the book to emphasis just how dangerous working on the docks could actually be.

Tony: "It's amazing. You've no idea how busy the docks were. It was the premier port. There were so many near misses down the docks that it's only now you realise just how dangerous it could be – so many tales."

This book has also been written in honour of the memory of the fine men Tony was privileged to come into contact with as a 'Day-Old Chick'. The dockers were much maligned by the media over the years and always reported as being militant and ready to strike over the least thing, when in fact every major industrial nation had more strikes than were experienced on the Liverpool docks.

It is the intention of the authors to bring to life the 'fantastic characters' who through sheer necessity tolerated many long, soul-destroying and poorly paid hours in what were often dreadful working conditions. Apart from the need to provide for their families, the dockers' humour helped them through. It was described as 'the humour of despair'. It was the humour of men struggling to live in substandard housing, work in a harsh industry, in a bankrupt country, pushing for change in the grey world of northern England; men whose work was classed as 'casual labour'; men who handled commodities that few could afford to put on their own tables.

There was hardly a home on Merseyside where there was not somebody concerned directly or indirectly with the port industry. Liverpool was one of the biggest and busiest ports in the world, and the natural gateway to America and the colonies of Australia and New Zealand, as well as Canada, and indeed the whole world. Every commodity imaginable was imported to, or exported from, this mighty city with its line of docks on the Liverpool side stretching seven miles from Seaforth to the Dingle, allied to the huge Birkenhead docks. Ships would anchor out in the river until there was room to get in it was that busy.

An army of men worked on the Liverpool docks, but thousands more were also concerned with ships and the sea. There were ship repair and maintenance, shipping offices and insurance, ship's chandlers, oil companies, the Royal Mail, railway workers, painting contractors, and steel and electric cable and instrument manufacturers, not to mention the tug boat crews and the police, who had their own specialised docks branch.

We hope that what follows will enlighten, enthral, and educate, but most of all entertain, and leave you with a greater understanding of a part of Liverpool's history that has gone forever.

Chapter 1
Dockers' Nicknames

Amid the hustle and bustle of a premier port, with all that was going on, and thousands of men employed there. Not just dockers themselves, but other workers as well. There was the shore gang, who did mostly the crew's job of getting the ship ready for sea, engineers from Campbell and Isherwood, post office engineers who put the phone lines in when ships first arrived, delivery drivers with food, tanker drivers with fuel, and myriads of people concerned with shipping. Because of this pot-pouris of characters, humour could bubble up at any time.

Nicknames

Dockers' nicknames were always a source of amusement, not only for the names themselves, but also how they were arrived at. If anyone stuck a nickname on you, the only way to get round it was by sticking a worse one on them. Some of the names were hysterical, but some could be downright cruel and insensitive.

One man had been badly injured in the First World War, and both his heels had been struck by shrapnel from an exploding shell; he walked around on his toes all the time and he was christened 'Horse Shoe Ned'. Another man had white side whiskers, a hump on his back and walked with his back arched, they nicknamed him 'The Angry Cat'.

One poor fella had no relatives and his wife had died. He was only in his late thirties and had little kids. He literally had nobody to look after them. Rather than them going into care, he did everything for them. He'd tell the men down the dock, 'Oh, am knackered'.

'Why, what's the matter?" they'd ask.

'Oh, av' been up all hours, 'ad te wash 'n iron the kid's clothes'.

Fellas got to know that his wife had died, and someone stuck the name 'Tommy Sad Tales' on him.

One day, someone not knowing the situation said, "Ye know wha' the' call you?'

'No. What?'

'Tommy Sad Tales', he replied.

The fella went ballistic and said, 'Tommy Sad Tales! My wife died, an' we've got no one. Am busy lookin' after me kids an' you stick a name on me? Who started the nickname? I'll stretch him right out'.

Nobody would admit to being the author of this particular 'handle'.

Most names were funny and harmed nobody. One docker had a load of kids and it seemed that he only had to hang his trousers up and his wife was 'off to the races'. He was called 'Fill the Cot'.

Another docker was given the title, 'The Lonely Baker', as he used to say, 'The kids are all married, so there's only me an' me tart left now'.

A docker going through a case of fashion shoes to get a pair for his wife said, 'I wonder if these'll fit her.

He was nicknamed 'The Diesel Fitter'.

Another fella was always saying, 'I wonder what's in tha' case. I wonder what's in tha' case'. He was called 'The Wonder Boy'.

A few dockers were known as liberty takers. One fella was always looking for an excuse to sneak away and have forty winks, sometimes in the shed or somewhere on the ship itself; he was called 'Bo Bo's'. At sometime, he was prosecuted for looking through his neighbour's windows on bath night, and when it was reported in the Liverpool Echo, his name was immediately changed to 'Bo Peep'.

There was a docker always sneaking away to the alehouse. The gang of dockers he'd be working with would say, 'Where's 'e gone? Oh, 'e 'asn't gone agen, 'as 'e?' They called him 'Vanishing Cream'.

One docker was given the nickname 'Francis Chichester' because he was always in the Atlantic (a pub). Amongst the liberty takers were those who looked for excuses to gain compensation. One man was always claiming for falling down some hole or another. They stuck the name 'The Rat' on him.

One of the most inventive nicknames was stuck on a fella who lived in Kirkby. His wife had bought him a khaki army overcoat to wear down the docks. There was a small cigarette burn in the back that looked for all the world like a bullet hole. It was noticed in the pen one morning, and everyone started to call him 'The Kirkby Coward'. Another docker also wore a khaki overcoat from the army and navy stores. He was very quiet and didn't mix much. Nobody actually knew his name, and he was called 'The Unknown Soldier'. Another fella always seemed to wear a dark blue rold neck sweater, so they named him 'The Frozen Sailor'.

A ship's boss came to work every day in a high crown hat. It looked like the old cowboy hats, so he became known as 'Cowboy Galvin'. Another fella would turn up at the docks in really smart clothes all the time. Someone called him the 'Hollywood Docker'.

There was a man called 'The Jelly', as he would say, 'One night an' I'll be set'.

One of the dockers absolutely hated working at the docks, and always moaned, 'Am bailin' outta this job. Am bailin' out of 'ere'. They named him 'The Windy Pilot'.

One lad worked normally with his dad, but sometimes they would be separated on different ships. They travelled home together and now and again the lad would come looking for his dad and be seen calling down different hatches, 'Is my old fella there?' With the Liverpool accent, it was pronounced, 'Me owl fella', like the meow of a cat. He was given the title 'The Windy Kitten', and it stuck.

Some people actually looked like the name that had been stuck on them. A lad from the south end worked at box one who had a thin face with a slightly hooked nose, and his eyes were too close together. He also had his hair cut in a crew cut, and instead of it being short, it stood up about four inches. When he walked, it flicked forward and backwards. It looked like a cock's comb. Someone said, 'He looks like a friggin' hen'. After that, he was always called 'The Hen'.

Another docker grew a goatee beard, which was unusual for that time, and he was named 'The Nanny Goat'.

Sometimes people used the nickname and forgot what their original names were. There was a holdsman called 'The Lemon Drop Kid' because he actually looked like a character in the kids' films. He fell down below on the west side into the lower hold of a ship. He landed on his head from quite a height and was completely unconscious. The dockers thought he was dead. When the ambulance man arrived, he asked what his name was. They all replied, 'Lemon Drop'.

'Don't ye know 'is real name?' the medic asked.

They all said, 'No. Everyone calls 'im 'The Lemon Drop Kid'.

No one actually knew his name, even though they'd worked with him for years. He was back at work a couple of days later. One docker said, 'Friggin' 'ell. He must 'ave 'ad a skull about three friggin' inches thick. Nobody I know could survive a fall like tha''.

Dockers would ask each other who were they working with, and they'd say things like,

'Erh, Vanishin' Cream. The Piano. The Hen. The Hollywood Docker. An', erh, Lemon Drop'. They'd just reel all the nicknames off as if it was the normal thing to do.

Among other nicknames were 'Paddy Kelly', 'Abraham Lincoln', and 'Little Boy Blue'. The latter was called this because he wore light-blue denim jacket and jeans and a blue cap. Paddy Kelly didn't have a nick name. His real name was Paddy Kelly. Men would shout his name along the quay to warn men who might be smoking that a policeman was approaching; it was just a coincidence. The tallest of the three was a lad who wore a Teddy Boy drape jacket that came almost to his knees. The jacket had a velvet collar, and he had a habit of standing with one hand at his side and the other clutching his lapel in a statesman-like manner. His posture was reminiscent of America's greatest president, and he was known as 'Abraham Lincoln'.

Most nicknames were thought up immediately something was done or said. At one ship, one of the dockers was always asking the rest of the gang, would they mind if he got away a few minutes early at dinner time, as his bus went dead on the hour, and if he missed it he'd have to wait twenty minutes for the next one. They had let him go on a few occasions but felt they were being taken advantage of, and nobody would look him directly in the eye.

He asked a few of the men if they would mind and then made the mistake of a lifetime. In desperation, he blurted out, 'Ar. 'Ey, lads. I've got te be away before twelve'.

The rest of the gang shouted out spontaneously and in unison, 'CINDERELLA!'

Of course the story went along the whole line of docks from the Gladstone to the Herculaneum and was passed on at the line of docks on the Birkenhead side.

One day, the ship's lifting gear was being used at one of the hatches on a Yankee boat. As the derricks were being moved, the man in charge called to a man holding a guy rope, instructing him to, 'Let that guy go'. He was promptly named 'The Lenient Judge'.

Another docker said that because he had an easygoing personality everyone took advantage of him. He complained, 'Everybody plays on me'. He quickly had the handle stuck on him 'The Piano'.

One docker asked his mate to do his work while he slipped away to the Irish Club for a pint. His mate refused, so he shouted over to him, 'I'll remember you,' (a sixties song). For years after he was known as 'Frank Ifield'.

There was a docker who had bright red hair. The fella had endured all the usual nicknames over the years: 'Ginger Nut', Red 'Ed' and so forth. One day, he went to Dirty Annie's cafe for his dinner. He asked this 'big fat boiling piece', with corn beef legs and greasy hair snatched back in a bobble, who was serving, for steak pie and chips.

'Ye too late, lad', she replied. 'Thee's no chips left'. The fella complained how rubbish the cafe was, as it never seemed to have anything he wanted.

The woman was annoyed and remarked, 'It's tuff luck, an' if ye don't like it, then get 'ere earlier or go somewhere else instead'.

The next day he went to the café. He stood at the counter, and true enough, the boiling piece was there. Again, he asked for steak pie and chips. She took one scathing glance at him, and before he could say another word, she shouted, 'Fuck off, CARROT'! Y'iv shit it'. All the dockers in earshot collapsed with laughter, and from that moment, everyone knew him as 'Carrot'.

The other women who worked in the dock canteens were given their share of insults. One docker referred to some fat woman who worked on the till as 'Havin' an arse like a bag of sand an' a nose like a blind cobbler's thumb'.

Another woman working there who thought she was God's gift but had bad acne was described as 'Havin' a face like a welder's bench'.

Some nicknames were used to describe sections of the work force. Gerry Gittens hired for Reas Berth and dockers regularly working there were known as 'Gittens Kittens'. Likewise, people who worked at Smiths on the west side were called 'Smith's Crisps'. 'China Skins' were in the majority, as this was the busiest berth in the whole of the Gladstone complex and there were nearly always two ships being discharged there. A group of men who lived near the Gladstone Dock and who came from Seaforth were collectively known as the 'Seaforth Highlanders'.

In the late '50s, the BBC decided to televise a show from the deck of the Empress of Canada, which was berthed at the CPR Berth in the Gladstone Dock. Several well-known entertainers were to perform, among them Shirley Bassey and a television personality named Hughie Green. The latter was a household name because of his talent show *Opportunity Knocks*, and other TV shows and panel games. One of the dockers who'd actually been to stage school as a child, had met Hughie and constantly reminded others of this fact.

The berth was busy with outside broadcast vehicles and equipment, and it was quite an exciting thing at the time. Dockers kept their eyes out for the personalities to arrive at the ship, and presently Shirley Bassey and Hughie Green turned up at the ship in a limousine. The docker was in the act of going to make a 'Billy' can of tea with a fist full of cups when he saw them getting out of the car down the quay. He put the can and cups down by a column and ran down the quay shouting, 'Hughie Green. Hughie Green', as they walked up the gangway and into the ship.

He was stopped from going aboard even after insisting that he'd known Hughie personally years before. No amount of explaining would allow him to board the ship, and he returned disgruntled to find that somebody had stolen his can and cups. Forever after, he was known as 'Hughie Green'.

It wasn't just the nicknames that were funny. There was sometimes a descriptive way the dockers spoke peculiar to themselves, which explained things in a few simple words. A window cleaner had suffered a fall when his ladder slipped away under him. Someone who witnessed it was talking about it the next day; he described the poor man as coming down 'Like a friggin' bomb'. Anybody who had overexerted himself and was out of breath would describe himself as 'Blowin'

11

for tugs'. And nothing ever broke; it always 'carried away'. These were nautical expressions, which were embedded in everyday speech on the Merseyside docks.

Not all instances or conversations ended up as a name to stick on someone. A holdsman who'd boxed professionally in his time without much success, in spite of promise as an amateur, was asked to settle an argument as to how many lights were over the ring in the Liverpool stadium.

'How would I know that?' He inquired.

A voice floated across the lower hold from someone in the second gang. 'Well, ye lay flat on ye back lookin' up at them enough times, didn't ye?'

Chapter 2
Skits, Wits, 'n'
Devilment

Dockers could be very quick witted and extremely
funny; they were always ready for a laugh. Some
terrible skits worked on the docks, and devilment
was rife. One docker chalked on the back of his
mate's Donkey jacket 'Happy Larry, that's me',
and his mate walked around all day wearing the
jacket not knowing anything about it. Another
docker was telling someone that his friend had
been off work for three weeks, 'with a broken
flask'. A docker talked of a fella who kicked a
tortoise because it'd been following him around
all day.

Some people could be hysterically funny, and
their quotes went along the line of docks like
wildfire. A heated political argument in a Scotland

Road pub one Sunday led to one docker (of Irish extraction himself), blurting out to an Irishman, 'If it wasn't for ye colour, you'd be the most hated race on earth'.

Sometimes at the gate in the lunch hour there would be people speaking politics to anybody who'd listen. One communist sympathizer was talking about complete nuclear disarmament by Britain. A group of young men were idly standing there listening when one of them spoke up.

'Ave I got this right? You wan' us te get rid of our nuclear deterrent? How about all the other weapons? One atomic bomb is the same as a thousand bomber raid, so to be killed by an atom bomb, or a conventional bomb, or a bullet, or a bow and arrow, or even a sock full of shit still makes ye dead. What's the difference?'

'Ahhhh', the orator replied, 'but with conventional weapons, y'id 'ave a chance te ge' away'.

Dockers were never comfortable with 'Jobsworths' (someone who is over zealous in their job). A docker from box one had an altercation with a snooty female desk clerk in a government department. As he walked out of the office, he shouted back to her, 'You're so fuckin' ugly ye should be fed with a catapult'.

A young docker with a couple of kids had got himself into trouble. He wasn't a bad lad, just young and a bit silly. The magistrate in Bootle gave him the option: 'Fined twenty pounds or a month in jail'. The magistrate told him that he would give him time to pay, but in the event of the fine not being paid, he certainly would 'do the month'. The young men replied, 'I'll do the fuckin' month'.

Big Fat Tractor Tyres

People did some hysterical things. At one time, part of the China Berth caught fire and molten rubber was running out of the shed and down the quay. Some bright spark thought he would ride his bike through it so that his tyres would be coated and last longer. He rode carefully through the stream of molten rubber and it certainly did coat the tyres. The problem was that it kept building up and when he got to the other side the rubber had solidified and the tyres looked as if they'd just come off a tractor. The tyres were too fat to revolve between the forks and he had to buy two new ones.

Stinky Scent in the Pen

Two young dockers had signed on at the pen because there was no work available that morning.

At a loose end, they decided to get a bus into Liverpool and walk around before they returned to the pen at one o'clock. They happened to walk down Moorfields in the city centre, and went into the 'Wizards Den', which was a joke shop that was well known to Liverpudlians. They bought a bottle of 'Stinky Scent' each, to have some fun later. The writing on the bottles proclaimed boldly that one of the ingredients was 'old army socks'.

It was a warm day, and there was no work available, so they had to 'sign on' again, and queued to pass the small window where their books would be stamped with an 'AP' (attendance proved) so they would be paid fall back pay even though they were not needed. As always happened, people started to push to get out of the Pen quicker, and what started as an orderly line degenerated into a mass of men trying to push through a small one-way gate that could only accommodate one person at a time.

One of the young dockers with the Stinky Scent decided to take the top off his bottle as he was in the centre of the crush; this would normally be sufficient to release the nauseating odour. With it being warm and with the crush of bodies increasing the temperature, he fumbled with the bottle, intending to unscrew the top momentarily, but found it was nigh impossible to screw the top back on and dropped it. The contents quickly dripped out, and the most sickening smell rose immediately to envelope the crowd. A huge roar went up: 'Jesus, Mary, and Joseph', and men tried to scatter to get out of the way. Some of the older dockers took their false teeth out and were retching with the smell. Men in the crush were stretching their necks to get their noses clear, and some dockers on the periphery of the crowd were leaning on the wall of the Pen with their heads down, baulking and nearly throwing up. The control officer came out of the office, got a waft of it, and hurriedly went back in, closing the door behind him. He re-emerged seconds later with a handkerchief over his mouth and nose and opened the main doors so fresh air could flood in. The crowd spilled into the sunshine, gulping in the fresh air. It took a while for everybody to recover.

The young dockers who'd caused the disruption kept quiet. They meant only to spread a faint waft through the Pen as a bit of a lark; they hadn't expected such a violent reaction. It took several hours with the doors and windows in the building open to be clear of the smell. The dockers talked about it for a long time afterwards.

Embarrassment Money

The West Gladstone Dock was a place where big ships loaded up for the Colonies, Australia, New Zealand, and so forth. Every conceivable type of product was exported from there, especially building materials, steel pipes, electrical products, and even bricks. A lot of plumbing equipment was also included: wash hand bowls and baths, taps, and copper pipes with every type of fitting imaginable. Among all this were toilet bowls. These were sent down below in a huge box packed with straw in between the layers to prevent breakage. The boxes used had a red cross painted on the side to denote a medical use, and doubled up as a way of getting injured men out of the hatch with the crane. The cry, 'Send a box down', would turn the head of anyone within earshot, who would wonder who had been hurt and how serious it was.

The dockers saw the toilet bowls as an excuse to squeeze extra money from their employers, and threatened strike action if they didn't receive 'embarrassment money'. They were given sixpence a day extra for the humiliation they claimed they felt. This claim was from fellas who'd seen a lot in their lives, who'd gone through a war, many of them in the Army or Merchant Navy, so the word embarrassment hardly came into their vocabulary.

One particular day, a box came down below filled with toilet bowls. The men started to lay the top layer of straw down under the combings and stack the bowls on top, followed by more straw. A line of dockers soon formed, lifting the bowls out one at a time and carrying them to where they were being stowed. Suddenly, one fella who'd just taken one from the box turned his head sideways, let out a gasp, and threw the bowl back into the box.

'Jeeeeez. God almighty', he gasped.

He walked away across the hatch and bent over with his head bowed and his hands on both knees, coughing his guts up, and spitting out in disgust. The other men looked into the box to see what had disgusted him. A roar of laughter erupted. Somebody had defecated in the toilet, and when it was lifted out more laughter erupted. On the side of the toilet was pencilled, and clearly visible for all to see, the legend, 'TESTED IN LIVERPOOL!

I'll Show Me Arse

Cassius Clay was to fight Sonny Liston, and holdsmen down below at a city boat in the West Alex Dock were arguing about who would win.

They were comparing the two fighter's abilities, and it got a bit heated. One guy from Seaforth got so worked up that he blurted out,

'If Clay beats Liston tonight I'll show ye me arse down the 'atch tomorra'.

Clay won, and the next morning the dockers were working when one of them remembered the bet. 'Eh, Tommy, are ye gonna show us ye arse?' he asked.

Tommy resigned himself to the fact that he'd have to comply and groaned.

'I knew some bastard would remind me', he complained.

He undid his pants and let them drop around his ankles, slid his underpants down, and bent over to expose his bare arse. A huge 'Ooooooooooooooh' erupted at the beautiful pair of boxer shorts he'd put on that morning. They were silk and grey with a floral pattern on them. He'd obviously come prepared, and his face broke into a broad grin.

'I might have known you buggers wouldn't forget', he said. He pulled his pants back up, fastened his belt, and hooked the next sling of bags onto the crane. 'Heave a bit, driver', he said.

Burnt Bottoms

The so-called toilets down the docks had not been designed originally for use as toilets. It seemed they'd been added as an afterthought to the sheds being built. The one at the back of the China Berth consisted of a sewage pipe with bolt holes around the perimeter of larger holes as a provision to bolt other pipes to. Partitions were built around every trap to afford some privacy, and a stream of water ran through the pipe constantly.

The trick was to wait for someone to use the toilet, and when they were seated, a newspaper would be rolled into a big ball, set fire to, and placed down the end opening. This would float along the pipe and flames would erupt around the person having a 'pony and trap'. Screams of protest would follow, and it was a constant threat to anybody wanting to relieve themselves.

Dirty Annie's

Dockers knew a dock canteen situated between the China Berth and the Hornby Dock as 'Dirty Annie's'. Hundreds of dockers walked past it each day. Some wit had chalked a mock menu on the board outside the building that read:

Dirty Annie's

Salmonella 1/6d

Enteritis 1/9d

Typhoid free with every tea bought and a merry Christmas to all our readers!

As dockers approached the canteen, they'd stop to read it, cheering and laughing as they went on their way.

Wally's Wig

Wally was unusual for a Liverpool docker. He wasn't a scouser for a start, and spoke in a broad Lancashire accent. He was a friendly, easygoing fella who said he lived with his sister in Prescot on Merseyside and told people that he'd got a transfer from the docks in Manchester. Men didn't believe that was possible, but that's what he told everybody. He carried a bit of weight, and had a reddish sort of face with protruding teeth. 'He could bite your arse through a cane chair', as somebody said. Wally had lost his hair prematurely, which was a shame for a young fella and he wore a wig. He'd been in box one for a few weeks and had made friends with some of the dockers there.

'Bald Eagle' was a scream – a real practical joker – always looking for some angle. He had a bald head and a hooked nose, and he looked just like his nickname. One morning, the gang went for their 'tango' (tea) to Dirty Annie's canteen. Bald Eagle had primed one of the girls who worked behind the counter but hadn't been there long.

'Oh. Oh. Wally will just love you. A girl your age. Slim. Brunette. Glasses'.

The girl laughed and wondered who Wally was. Bald Eagle went back to the job after his tea break and told Wally that the new girl in the canteen had asked what his name was. Wally replied, 'Are yur sure it was me she was interested in? Are yur shuwer?'

'Definitely you, mate. Honest', he said.

Now, Wally always had an army haversack with him, slung across his body that the other dockers wondered about. It seemed a bit excessive that he should need something that size just to carry the odd sandwich in. It would soon become apparent why he carried it around with him constantly.

Lunchtime arrived and the gang went back to the same 'canny'. A queue of dockers lined up towards the counter from the door waiting to be served. The girl behind the counter recognised Bald Eagle and assumed that the docker with him must be the fella he'd mentioned earlier, and she glanced in their direction as she served people with food. The canteen was packed at that time of the day, and it was Wally's turn to be served.

Wally looked strangely different somehow. It was something you couldn't figure out at first, but there was something! Bald Eagle knew what it was. When they'd first arrived at the canteen door, Wally had walked around the side of the canny, out of view momentarily, and then rejoined Eagle in the queue. His hair looked neater and seemed more lustrous and had miraculously grown little short sideburns on it. The haversack contained Wally's best wig and he'd swapped it over.

Presently, they were being served and the girl in question blushed as Wally stood in front of her and placed his order. The next minute, he was holding a plate of pie chips and peas in his left hand and a mug of tea in his right with a side plate balanced on top of the cup with two rounds of bread and butter. There was a slight crush at the counter and Wally said to the girl in his thick Lancashire accent, 'Wally's the nerm'.

At that very moment Bald Eagle struck.

"Scuse me, Wal', he said as he reached around Wally and stretched to get a knife and fork from the box on the counter, making sure that he brushed his arm across Wally's forehead. In a flash, Wally's best wig turned sideways on his head and one of the little sideburns was hanging down over his nose. He couldn't do anything about it. His hands were full. He tried to put everything down on the counter so he could fix his wig but there was no room. He had to back out of the crush still balancing his dinner and put it down on the table before he could turn his wig back around.

An explosion of laughter erupted in the canteen and Wally was mortified! The girl was horrified! Bald Eagle apologised profusely.

'Ahhhhh. Am sorry, Wally. I didn't mean te do tha'. I was stretchin' for the knives an' forks and tha' an' just touched ye with me sleeve'.

Wally rumbled it right away. Bald Eagle turned and ran out of the canny as fast as he could. Wally followed him out to screams of laughter and started chasing him along the main avenue towards the Hornby gate with his hand on top of his head holding his best wig down, shouting, 'I'll kill you, yer basturd, when I get yur'.

Bald Eagle didn't come back to work that afternoon. He thought it might be better to give Wally time to cool down.

The Chase

Tommy's wife had had a liaison with a docker named Paddy. Not an affair as such, but she'd been out with her sister for a drink in the local pub and it was more of a quick fumble around the back. Tommy had been on nights and presently word got back to him. He knew Paddy – not well – but he was just one of the men who worked in the same pen. Paddy found out that Tommy was gunning for him and kept his eyes peeled in case he should bump into him. With working in such a confined area, it wasn't easy keeping out of the way and Paddy would be wary of going into the pen in case Tommy was there, as he had a strong aversion to being beaten up.

Soon after, they both met walking down the avenue at the back of the Colony Berth and Paddy flew for his life with Tommy after him, screaming what he would do to him when he got his hands on him. Over a period of weeks, several more instances occurred where Tommy nearly copped for him but Paddy, being fleet of foot, managed to get away. It clicked in Tommy's head one day that when he caught up with this gigolo he would give him a hiding and then it was over. He realised that he could make this fella's life a real misery by just chasing him and never catching him. Paddy would be forever condemned to looking around corners, terrified that Tommy might be near.

Paddy had friends who kept him informed of Tommy's whereabouts if they could and it filled his whole horizon. He thought of leaving the docks and trying to get a job elsewhere, but he couldn't really afford to do that, as he had a wife and kids to support. He would go for a pint at the weekend to some distant pub where there was no chance of bumping into his persecutor. At first, men down the docks would take an interest as Paddy came flying past with Tommy in pursuit but eventually it became such a commonplace sight that little or no interest would be taken.

Tommy always paced his pursuit carefully. He didn't want Paddy to rumble that the punishment was in the chase and would let Paddy stay just out of his grasp. Men would see Paddy running out of the back door of Dirty Annie's canteen as Tommy came in the front. Men would be drinking tea or playing cards and would hardly look up.

Eventually, Tommy and his family moved up to a new house in Skelmersdale, and Paddy could live a normal life as Tommy had got a new job up there. Paddy had learned his lesson, and for the first time in a year, he could walk about and go to work or for a pint without worrying who he would bump into. He never ever realised that Tommy had been chasing him all that time without real intent.

Anythin' Does for the Dock

Some dockers wore the most ragged clothes for work, but not all, and there was an expression used down at the docks: 'Anythin' does for the dock'. It wasn't unusual to see a holdsman wearing a coat tied with a piece of string around the middle and quite often men (particularly older dockers) wore a hat and belt buckle on the side. 'Checkers' usually dressed up more and some were quite smart, even wearing ties with white shirts, as their job was paperwork and they weren't exposed to dirty cargo.

One docker had been out to the shops to buy some bits and pieces in the dinner hour and on the way back to the ship was stopped and asked the time by another docker. He fumbled in the bag he was carrying, took out a tin of boot polish, looked at the lid, and told him, 'Ten te one'.

The man was puzzled and said, 'But that's a tin of boot polish'.

'Well, anythin' does for the dock', he replied.

Jaspers

On the China boats as the cargo was being unloaded, jaspers that look like big orange cockroaches – really ugly things – would scuttle down lower and lower until they'd be under the last layer of cargo on the bottom of the ship. When the timber was lifted up, they'd scatter everywhere and sometimes some of them would run really quickly along it towards men's hands.

A couple of dockers were lifting some timber and a fella was terrified of them. As one ran towards him he panicked, screamed, and dropped his end of the length of wood. It went like a bow string – Doyoidoyoiyong – and it nearly ripped the arms out of the other fella's sockets.

'Friggin' 'ell', the fella said. 'Wha' did ye do tha' for? Ye nearly broke me bleedin' arms ye soft shit 'ouse. What's the matter with ye? ye big girl's blouse'.

The other dockers who'd seen the commotion skittered him for ages afterwards.

Sinatra

One of the dockers fancied himself a crooner and knew all of Frank Sinatra's songs. He was constantly set up by the other dockers and never ever suspected. Sometimes in the shed, a tape measure or something else would be used to simulate a microphone and one of the other dockers would start to sing a Sinatra song. The others would gather 'round, feigning interest, and sure enough our man would appear and stand at the back, watching and listening.

Slowly but surely, he would edge his way toward the front, and when the time was right he would lunge and snatch the 'microphone' from whoever was singing and go off onto 'Fly Me to the Moon', or some other Sinatra hit. The dockers would start clicking their fingers in time as if they were really enjoying it. He would then go through a couple more songs while the audience kept their faces straight and shouted out requests for him to sing. His eyes would be lit up and he would be flinging his arms out as he imagined 'Ol' Blue Eyes' would do in Las Vegas. He never imagined that when this impromptu performance was finished and the gang dispersed that some men would be crying with laughter in the dock shed. He was obviously named 'Frank Sinatra'.

Little Tiny Guy

There was a little tiny guy in box one known as Abey, who was of Eastern European ancestry. He was about five feet tall and very old. He looked like a cartoon character, with a big nose and big lips, and his face was full of blackheads that turned to crocuses every summer. He had something wrong with his leg. The man could hardly walk, let alone work. He normally got a job as 'Landing Man'. This was a job usually given to older men, as all they had to do was unhook slings as they were lowered to the quay, although sometimes he would be in a gang where he had to lift heavy bags or something similar, and the man was incapable of doing that.

From time to time, Abey would pay younger men to do his work for him. Men would watch him walking down the shed with the peculiar gait he had. He would take three steps and the fourth would be a little sort of stumble. Dockers would say, 'Watch this', and call out in time, 'One, two, three, whip. There ye go', and laugh as Abey did his little dance, unaware he was being watched. Dockers used to say that if Abey was in your gang, you were a man short right away.

Stan's Kecks

A little, short, fat fella named Stan was the manager of a pub on the Dock Road. Stan would wear huge half-mast pants that had a waistband finishing just under his chest, which left a little gap for his tiny braces. He would come 'round collecting glasses, saying, 'Time please, gentlemen'.

The dockers would all look at Stan and snigger at the sight of him. One fella said, "Ave ye seen the state of 'is bloody kecks? They're friggin' huge'.

Another lad said, 'I wunder wha' size chest his kecks are'.

Some other wit added, 'He looks like Mr Five by Five, Five foot tall and friggin' five foot wide'.

Howls of laughter erupted in the pub and poor Stan would smile over at the dockers as if to say he was glad they were enjoying themselves, not knowing they were laughing about him.

The Phantom Coat Thief

One retired docker called Eddie was well into his 70s but still drank in one of the Dock Road pubs. Eddie's mind had gone; he'd get confused and forget things, or he'd do some bizarre things. His son, who was also a docker, would tell the lads what Eddie had been up to. He'd say, 'I found a mouldy loaf in the gas cupboard the other day, an' a pan of peeled spuds with slugs in it 'round the back of the shed. Me ma said, 'I wondered where the pan 'ad gone, an' I knew I'd bought an extra loaf last time I went shoppin'. Oh, that's ye bloody dad again. I think his mind's goin'. He's been doin' things like tha' for weeks'.

One evening, Eddie was in the pub, sitting reading a newspaper, or so everyone thought. One fella noticed that it was upside down and just chuckled to himself. Eddie had been sitting there for a while with a ciggy stump in his mouth, unlit, just staring at the paper. The next minute, he got up to go home and made his way over to a chair where a couple of dockers' coats had been left and he put on the two coats. One was far too long and it trailed on the floor as he walked out. One docker had noticed him and shouted, 'Eddie, you've got the wrong coat on'.

Eddie just shouted, 'Fuck off', and continued on his way home. The fella thought the scenario was hysterical and left Eddie to it. When the other men found their coats missing they went mad. The docker who knew the score told them what had happened.

A short while later, Eddie's wife, Rose, noticed a couple of coats draped over the banister rail in the hall and wondered how they'd arrived there. She realised that Eddie had brought them home from the pub and she ran straight 'round there to hand them back. The men were given their coats, and for a long time after, all the dockers kept their coats close by, just in case the 'Phantom Coat Thief' struck again.

Big Fat Pantomime Bobby

As a rule, the police were disliked intensely. It was well known by seafarers that you could get more than your allotted amount of purchased cigarettes out of the gate merely by putting a couple of half crowns under your receipt from the chief steward and handing it to the bobby as you passed through the gate. Pubs in Liverpool kept on the right side of them too.

A docker from down the line found out that the local pub landlord used to leave a pint bottle of beer on the wall at the back of the pub for a big fat police sergeant when he'd be around in the middle of the night. He was known as the

'Pantomime Bobby', and he was hated by all and sundry. This man's house overlooked the back of the pub and he kept watch.

He soon found out what time this fool would be around, and one night sneaked out and got the bottle and drank the beer himself and put the empty bottle back on the wall. He then defecated at the foot of the wall and went back into his house to listen to what would happen.

True to form, the sergeant turned up and took off his hob nailed boots so he could sneak around the back without being heard. The man listened as the policeman picked up the bottle and found it was empty. He lay in bed listening to the quiet cursing from the back entry and could hardly stop himself screeching with laughter as he heard the cry of revulsion as the Bobby stood right in the shit in his stocking feet. He never found out who was responsible. The story went around like wildfire and everybody was delighted that at last this bastard had got his comeuppance.

The Double Decker Drunk

One time, a docker on a night out got really drunk. He had the bright idea of stealing a double-decker bus to get home. The only thing was, he lost his way, so he pulled up right outside of the police station and asked for directions. At court, the magistrate asked if he wished to say anything.

'Beam me up, Scottie', he replied.

Chapter 3
Skiving on the Job

The Dockers' Tea Party

Rolls Royce cars were being loaded at the Yankee Berth. The cars were left open because of the need to manoeuvre them, although the batteries and carburettors were locked in the boots. Beautiful and expensive crockery was stacked under the combings, and a night gang making tea found out that they didn't have enough cups.

One man found that he could squeeze his hand through the wire mesh and straw that the cups were packed in, and he did this a few times to get some cups out. The tea was made and two dockers were sitting in the back of a Rolls with their legs crossed, sipping the brew with these beautiful little cups held between thumb and forefinger with their little fingers cocked up in an exaggerated manner. The guy with the big tin of tea leaned in.

'More tea, m'lud?' he said, inciting gales of laughter.

'And when we've finished, would you return the cups to the scullery?' he added, to more laughter.

They duly returned the cups to the straw-filled crates, complete with tea leaves. God knows what the reaction was when they arrived at some prestigious chain store in New York.

Father Christmas Down Below

One fella called Charlie got a job as a dock porter. On his first day, he had to go down below and finish discharging, as there was a little bit of cargo left on the ship. They were also loading bales of charity clothes on the ship that had been collected from all over Britain – good coats, shoes, pants, shirts, and so on.

Charlie climbed down the hatch and couldn't believe it. There was a fella with a full Father Christmas outfit on – the big robes, with the white fur trim, and the beard – sitting there playing the piano. The dockers had made a bar out of cases and they had optics with bottles in just like the pub. The fellas said to Charlie, "Ere y'ar'. Come an' 'av a bevy lad. Ye got ye gin, ye got ye rum, ye got ye whisky'.

The dockers were all leaning on the bar, having a ciggy, which was strictly illegal. You'd get nicked for smoking on the quay, never mind down the ship. The ship's mate would tell the police; ships easily go on fire. Dragging on ciggies, they were all standing round having a little drink. 'Help ye selves, lads. Je want whisky?'

Charlie thought someone was taking the Mickey. Looking around, he said, 'Father Christmas is playin' the piana, an' they've got a bar down below, me first mornin' actually workin' on the docks'.

'Am sure people think am lyin', but it's the God's honest truth'.

Excuses

A docker from number one pen had to go to see the boss, 'Ted Bell', over at box two. He'd missed a job in the morning and another man was hired to take his place. He now had to face the headman and explain why he hadn't turned in that morning.

'I couldn't 'elp it', he explained. 'I was in plenty of time, bu' when I went te get me bike out, it 'ad a puncture. I still 'ad enough time te fix it an' get te the job. I took the valve out an' let the rest of the air out so I could ge' the tube out from the tyre. I stuck a patch on the tube, bu' took the valve rubber off the valve te 'ave a close look a' it, te see if it was okay. I was puttin' the tube back in te the tyre before pumpin' it up, an' pu' the valve rubber on the floor. Anyway, I keep hens, an' ye wouldn't believe it, one of the hens must 'ave thought it was a worm an' et it, just like tha'. I didn't 'ave another valve rubber, so couldn't ride me bike te werk, an' that's why I missed the ship'.

Ted Bell kept his face straight, mulling this over. Through the years, he thought he'd heard every excuse under the sun – people being ill, missing the bus, having a bad pint the night before, and so on. He thought for a few seconds, looking at this fella in front of him with his cap in his hand. The seconds passed with Ted staring at him. Presently, he pursed his lips and said simply, 'Okay', and allowed him to go without punishment. The docker went back to number one pen and told his mates about it.

'He let me off', the docker said, 'but somethin' must 'ave amused 'im, cos when I was leavin' the buildin', I could 'ear 'im laughin' in his office'.

The Welt

The welt was a system of half a gang going off the job while the rest of the gang worked without them. On their return, the others would then disappear for an hour – 'An hour about'. On some jobs, men would work half a day about, or even a day about. In some circumstances, this could not be avoided, as holdsmen might be busy down below moving dunnage (odd pieces of timber) or rigging gin blocks up to pull a heavy case under the combings and out of the square of the hatch. Consequently, there was no cargo being loaded or discharged and men on the quay would drift off to the canteen instead of waiting by the door of the shed. The welt was an integral part of dock work, and tended to suit everybody.

The practice of working the welt would nearly always be carried out, busy or not, and in most cases employers liked this setup because they could blackmail the men into working harder and breaking the rules even if it was dangerous. With a rope sling, the most that's supposed to be lifted in one is eighteen hundredweight, and sometimes a hatch boss would see a sling going up out the hatch and shout down, 'Fill them slings up, lads'.

Someone would shout that there were eighteen bags in the sling, and he'd shout down, 'Yeah, and there's four men in the alehouse'.

As a rule, employers would not complain if the work was being done; it was only when the steel wire (the fall) from the crane was seen to be inactive that action was taken and the men were threatened with sending the timekeeper around to find out who was missing. So, to save him fetching the timekeeper 'round, you had to overload every sling. Slings with over thirty bags were often seen going up out the hatch, and the rope that would normally be the width of a man's wrist would become the size of a thumb. When the crane heaved, the sling would stretch like an elastic band and oil could be seen coming out the rope, which would get on your hands. You never stood under one of those.

Some jobs had to be worked using the welt system. On meat boats, the holds were refrigerated and it was deemed that an hour down below in freezing temperatures was the most a man could bear before getting hypothermia or frostbite. There was never any provision for the issue of protective clothing, and working an hour about was accepted practice.

Ships' cargos were piecemeal and dockers could be handling thousands of small boxes in the morning when all hands were needed for the job. The commodity coming up might then change to big heavy cases in the afternoon, where the runabout crane on the quay would be used to do the work; so a pool of labour would be employed,

(Usually eight men when discharging and four when loading.)

The problem sometimes arose that someone might go to the pub on his hour off and get too comfortable. They would then leave a man doing his job, often until seven o'clock that night – six hours straight through. This was known as 'working it up ye'. It was an unwritten law that if it happened to you, even if the timekeeper came around, you kept the job going as best you could to cover his absence. Anybody 'working it up' anybody else was scorned by the rest of the men. It was one of the worst things you could do, and people had long memories.

On some ships, the employers had to hire the right number of men in a gang, even if the cargo didn't need that many, and men arranged it between themselves to work a day about. At one job, the holdsmen had arranged for one man to stay down below while the other three went for a bevvy. It was that kind of job where all he had to do was hook the crane on and they would not be needed for hours.

There wasn't any hold up in the cargo coming ashore, but the hatch boss decided to tell the timekeeper, who came and shouted down the hatch, 'Give us ye numbers, lads'.

The man hooking on down below could be seen in the square of the hatch, and he shouted his number up. He walked back under the combings and reappeared with his cap and an overcoat on, pretending to be someone else and shouted another number out, which the timekeeper duly noted. He then went out of sight again under the combings and came out minus a cap and his sweater and called yet another number up. The timekeeper ticked this off and when he emerged for the third time and pretended to be adjusting a sling around a case and kept his face turned away so he wouldn't be recognised and shouted the last number half over his shoulder, the timekeeper rumbled him and burst out laughing. The timekeeper must have been all right, because the job wasn't stopped. He marked them all as present and walked away with his shoulders shaking.

Tell Ye Sister

Two young fellas started work on the docks. Both had shoulder-length hair, which was a new thing in the early sixties. They soon got into the accepted routine of working an hour about, and followed the dockers' routine of going for a pint in their hour off. The problem was that the Irish Club was warm and comfortable, and after a couple of pints, people forgot the time. One of them was going back to the ship and the other said he'd follow on. As the first fella walked down the quay, the ship's boss knew he'd been away from the job and shouted down from the deck of the ship.

"Ey, you. You're cleared out. An' tell ye sister she is too'.

Chapter 4
Dockers 'n' Bosses

Abraham Lincoln

Some dockers were in awe of nobody; they held little regard for status, position, or power. One day, Abraham Lincoln was standing near a dock shed when the big boss turned up in his posh car. Out stepped a very tall, slim gentleman, finely dressed in a suit and bowler hat. In his beautiful English speaking voice, he politely asked Abraham, 'Young man, have you no work to do?'

Abraham wasn't at all fazed by the man and replied, 'Erm, well, ye see, mister, I've been waitin' for ye te come an' stretch te ge' me ball off the roof'. (The roof was about a hundred feet high.)

Boxed In

At box three, naked cars were being loaded as opposed to 'case cars', which were in bits and packed into big cases. The cars were parked along the avenue at the back of the shed, and some were by the fence at the Dock road end of the shed.

The ship's boss wasn't liked at all. Men realised that some discipline had to be enforced, but this man was a real snarler who gave no quarter. Cars had been going into the ship all day, being lifted one at a time on the special jig and sent down below. The boss had a car himself, which he parked at the end of the berth. Late in the afternoon, someone approached him and told him his car wasn't in its normal place and asked him if he'd parked it somewhere else. He told them that he hadn't and went to look. Sure enough, it was gone. He spent some time looking around the berth, and walked through the shed to check but to no avail. He'd never parked it anywhere else, so knew he couldn't be mistaken.

He started to get upset and wondered if it had been stolen. Maybe it had been moved, he thought. He went through the shed and boarded the ship to ask if anybody knew where it was. The hatch boss at number three hatch was leaning and looking down the hatch, and as the ship's boss approached, he nodded down towards the lower hold. The ship's boss looked down and nearly choked. There in the square of the hatch surrounded by brand new cars was his Ford Anglia. The dockers had loaded it for Australia and it was well and truly boxed in.

He stormed around, shouting for the men to get it out again and threatened anyone in earshot with the sack. He was fuming, and remarkably the gang who'd sent it in was looking as innocent as only they could. He stumbled down the gangplank and went up to the men who were pushing another car onto the lifting jig.

'Whose idea was this?' he demanded.

The men looked at each other, keeping their faces straight.

'You must have known it wasn't cargo', he said to the nearest man in the gang. 'It's obvious. It's even got a tax disc on the bloody windscreen. Start unloading those cars now, and get mine out'.

The dockers sent the jig down below to start reversing the loading process and the boss stormed off to the office; as soon as he disappeared, the men on the deck and quay and down below burst out laughing in unison. All this must have had some effect because it was noted that his attitude mellowed slightly over the next few days. Dockers didn't suffer tyrants readily, and this was a taste of what they could do!

The 'Pen'

The Gladstone Dock pen was just inside the Gladstone gate on the right. The proper name was the Control, but it was rarely called that. It was a low brick building with small frosted glass windows high up. Its entrance was a set of double doors at one end, and there was an exit only gate at the other end, which made a loud clacking noise when somebody passed through. It was like a hall inside, with markings on the floor to denote which category of docker stood to be hired. The doors were locked at 8 A.M., and a boss would emerge from the office with the control officer to start hiring holdsmen, porters, deckhands, or checkers.

The men would line up on the marks, facing one way usually, and the boss would walk down the line, touching men on the shoulder who would then pass their 'book' to his timekeeper following up behind. The men knew the bosses and which firm they were hiring for, so some jobs were much sought after while others were not.

The China Berth was the most disliked. It was nearly always discharging rubber bales. These were coated with French chalk to stop them sticking together, but with the tremendous weight in a hold, they often fused together and sometimes had to be 'dogged' and pulled out one at a time with a crane. The rubber was hoisted out in nets, seventeen at a time, and sometimes swung into the loft thirty feet above the quay where it was trucked into different parts of the shed by a team of porters. It was soul-destroying work, extremely boring, and potentially very dangerous. From time to time, there were instances of bales falling out of the net and landing on the quay below. They weighed about 160 pounds, and would bounce down the quay, emitting puffs of French chalk, while men in the vicinity literally ran for their lives as these things followed them, as if they had a mind of their own.

Dockers' wages were made up mostly of overtime. Four seven o'clocks were normal at the China, but it was hard earned money, and there were rarely ever any Sunday shifts. On the other hand, the firms at the west side were loading boats, paying over and above the normal rates by awarding 'tonnage', and working Sundays as well as four sevens, often putting night gangs on – even on Saturday nights when the overtime rate quadrupled.

If you worked on the loading boats, the money was terrific. Dockers would be paid three times the wage. The cargo would often be case cars or steel pipes, and there was often no need to handle anything manually. Although a greater weight of cargo was shifted on the west side, it was easier work and paid more money even for the same hours worked at the China.

When the control officer came out of the office with one of Smith's bosses, the men would push toward them, hoping to be hired. Sometimes the crush would get too much and the control officer would appeal for order and even threaten the men by saying, 'Stop breaking the stand up or I'll fetch the China out'.

If the China boss was hiring, men would avoid him by walking off the stand or dipping their shoulder down to avoid being touched by him and thereby hired. In some cases, men would walk out through the non-return gate to avoid this happening and would take the risk of being punished by suspension. The men then wouldn't have their book stamped with AP (Attendance proved). If they had a blank space, they'd have to go to Ted Bell in box two to get told off and warned, but they reckoned it was better to lose a day's pay than to get stuck on the China for a week.

One morning, the fella who hired for the China Berth came out of the pen to pick the men and they all recognised him. There was a big scatter to get out of the way. Fellas would literally dip their shoulder as he went to touch them, and he'd say, 'Give us ye book', and they'd be running 'round the pen, and he'd be running after them, shouting, 'Give us ye book!'

One man in the excitement appeared to have a heart attack and collapsed on the floor. Immediately, he was surrounded by men who wanted to carry him outside into the fresh air to have a legitimate excuse for walking out of the pen to avoid being hired. The man concerned was slight of build, but it took eight men to lift him up and walk out of the control. As they passed, one opportunist reached over and pinched one of the man's bootlaces between his finger and thumb as if he was taking some of the weight. He walked out with them, and even the control officer burst into laughter. That lunch hour, the expected loading boat docked on the west side, and the men who'd avoided the dreaded China that morning were in the pen, and were hired and looked forward to a big week.

One time, a boss was hiring for a week of five o'clocks. There was an obvious aversion to being caught, and he called out to men sliding along the wall of the pen, 'Come on, lads. Make a shape'. One wit stood to attention and then put his hands on his hips and stuck his elbows out from his sides and shouted back, 'How's that for the FA Cup?'

The very next morning, they were hiring men for a week of nights at a Yankee boat and the same fella was pushing with others to be hired. The control officer said something to the man hiring and he duly picked everybody except the wit from the day before. He was left standing alone in the pen. As the control officer walked back to his office, he called back over his shoulder, 'And how's that for a lighthouse!'

Elephant on the Wire

They built pens on the deck of the ship so that the livestock could get fresh air. The story was that elephants had come over with other animals. The trick was that the elephants had to be lifted onto the quay from the ship. An elephant was coming off a ship, and the dope who had to sling it up took a wire called a goods wire, which is about as thick as your little finger. Well, to an elephant, that's like a razor blade. The fella threw the sling underneath and round the elephant, hooked it on to the crane, and said, 'Heave a bit, driver'.

The crane driver heaved. They should have used a big canvas nappy like a tent to spread the weight out, but they didn't. When they heaved away, they cut the elephant in half.

Now, that was the story, but the other story that did actually happen was, the checker was marking off the elephants, and seemingly there were five elephants. As one went ashore, he marked a little line – one elephant, next line, two elephants. When he has four lines, he draws a bar through them so he can go five and count. He must have been talking to someone and forgot to put the bar through the four vertical lines. The boss said, 'Er, how many elephants are there?'

The checker said, 'Four'.

So the boss said, 'Well, there's five on the quay. How on earth can ye miss a friggin' elephant? Isn't it big enough! You've only got five te count, an' you've counted them wrong.' The boss continued, 'You've said there's four, and there's friggin' five gone ashore'.

And it went down: the checker who'd missed the elephant.

Ink Splatter

One of the hatch bosses, 'Alf,' got a gang, not a hatch, but a job in charge on the quay at the China Berth. He wouldn't have to get his hands dirty, so came to work in his best clothes – his best cap and Gabardine mac, and his best shoes, highly polished. He was an elderly man near retirement who'd been on the docks for years. He'd had a slight stroke a couple of years before, and it had left him with one side of his mouth drooping down.

Rubber bales were to be discharged and lifted by the crane up into the loft where a line of men would truck them to various piles. A man was designated to mark the bales with a purple ink that was always used. There was a technique used when marking the bales as a constant spray no matter how minute, over a ten hour working day would have a cumulative effect, leaving the man doing the marking covered in the stuff. People marking always brushed away from themselves. A number three, for example, was an oblique line with a dot above and below it. Close to it, it seemed to make no sense but standing back a couple of feet made it clear.

The floor of the loft and some parts of the whitewashed wall had numbers written on them in preparation for the bales, which now, first thing in the morning, were being swung in by the crane and the line of men were starting to truck the rubber in while looking for the numbers that matched their particular bale. The loft was divided into sections with wide doorways, and because of the amount of cargo, more than one section was marked out.

Alf was busy organising things, and he was constantly referring to sheets of paper. He was talking to the man who was marking out the areas for stowage, and had a small paintbrush and a big tin of the ink in his hand, suspended by a wire handle. When Alf had explained something to the man, they both turned around to walk away and both realised that they needed to ask something and spun around to face each other again – with disastrous consequences. They bumped into each other violently with the big tin of purple ink between them. It went off like a depth charge. There was a huge purple spray that covered the two of them, and Alf, dressed in his best gear with his cap set at a jaunty angle, was drenched in it. It caught him on the face and chest, and splattered all over his best mac and shoes.

There was a stunned silence from the men around them. The man holding the empty tin hadn't caught it as bad as Alf, and besides, was in his old working clothes. He was trying to speak but it seemed he couldn't get the words out. Poor Alf, his glasses were now opaque and he removed them carefully so he could see while still holding his bundle of papers and attempted to pull a handkerchief from out of his coat pocket. His mouth seemed to have drooped a little more than usual and he uttered quietly but loud enough for the men to hear, 'Fuckin' 'ell. Fuckin' 'ell'.

With as much dignity as he could muster under the circumstances, he turned and walked towards the stairs that led down to the lower level.

The minute Alf got through the door, the men hissing with suppressed laughter, with bloated red faces, burst into screams, and four of the men were draped over some bales of rubber, completely helpless with mirth. The man with the now empty ink tin was red with embarrassment, but he too couldn't hold it all in and started to laugh. An idea struck him. 'Where do you get more ink from?' he asked. Some wit chipped in, 'Try the pen'.

The mirth rose to a higher level. Alf had to go home and change into his normal ragged dock clothes, and came back after the lunch hour to his gang who had to avert their eyes lest they should start laughing.

Frankie Dutton

Dutton was hysterically funny. He was working in the Gladstone Dock at the meat berth, and the man in charge was named Mr Lamb. For one reason or another, Mr Lamb had to leave the berth for a while and he took off his white coat and his cap and left them in the office. When he'd gone, most of the men lit cigarettes while standing at the gate by the quay.

Smoking in the shed or near the ship was a criminal offence, and could get you the dead sack and a prosecution to boot, so the men smoking glanced around warily. Meanwhile, Dutton sneaked into Lamb's office and donned his white coat and cap and even put on his horn-rimmed glasses he'd left behind. After a few minutes, conversations started up and the men relaxed a little. This was when Frankie chose to make an appearance, and he emerged from around the corner and caused instant mayhem. Everyone was extinguishing their cigarettes in haste until some wag recognised him and said, 'Don't panic, lads. It's only Dutton dressed as Lamb'.

Young Wit

About the same time, a lad from Huyton, who even at his tender years was a noted wit, was sent over to Cammel lairds in Birkenhead by the dole office to work as a painter's labourer. One of the nuclear submarines was nearing completion and there was work available. He arrived on his first morning and reported to the foreman, who asked him his name and where he came from, and then told him that work had been carried out high up on the side of the Conning tower, and that he would have to get up there and wire brush it and paint the bare metal with red lead.

The lad looked up and said, 'That's got to be forty foot up in the air'.

'Oh, don't worry', said the foreman. 'We'll send you up in a bosun's chair'.

'I wouldn't go up there in a three-piece suite', the lad quipped.

Chapter 5
Pilfering Down the Dock

Some called Liverpool the 'City of Thieves'. What they did not realise is that men had little or nothing, and often handled cargo they could only dream of affording. Pilfering down the dock was known as 'carrying out'.

Salmon 'n' Suits 'n' Whisky 'n' Tha'

Security was always stepped up when ships were berthed, especially when cargo of considerable value was being discharged and removed when ships departed. Men handled all kinds of cargo and became inured to its value. Salmon was a luxury and few could afford to buy it in the shops. A ship could be discharging thousands and thousands of cases of salmon and men would watch it being hauled from the hatches on boards, sixty to a hundred cases at a time, realising that their wives could not afford to put such a luxury on the table. Wagons would be seen driving over cans and would burst them, but if you touched them you'd be sacked. The odd can could be consumed 'down below' without the risk of going out through the main gate, or taken to the canteen and added to a plate of chips at dinner time.

One time, an elderly man stole a tin of salmon. He'd actually never stolen before, and was very religious, but he'd just been tempted this day. The man took the salmon and walked towards the dock gate, but just happened to be stopped by a bobby and was prosecuted. He went to court the next day for pilfering. The man was waiting a couple of days to go to 'Sefton House', which was the actual Dock Labour Board office. He would have lost his job on the dock, but the poor man was so ashamed that he went home, put a shilling in the gas, put his head in the oven, and gassed himself – tragic! They had to draw the line somewhere, and any pilfering at all was dealt with in the same way.

Although most of the cargo would be untouched by the men discharging it, there was, however, an element employed on the docks prepared to take the risk of being stopped at the gate and searched by the police, but they were in a minority. They would come over to a ship if they heard that 'something was going'. This was frowned upon by the men actually working at that hatch, watching them load up and disappear, only to return later when they'd sold it to a local shop or in the pub. There was a perverse sense of morality present, and most men frowned upon this behaviour. 'Liberty takers' were disliked intensely; their behaviour didn't fit in with what was acceptable.

Suit lengths were bolts of cloth, enough to make an average suit. They were normally marked down one edge 'For export only', but were sold easily around the pubs. There were enough small tailors around to make a suit up with no questions asked, and it was always beautiful fabric. With the British history and expertise in making cloth, it was one of our most prestigious exports and was in demand around the world. It was not unusual to go into a pub in Liverpool and see a docker having a pint, looking like he's just stepped out of a window in Saville Row.

Whisky was the most desirable thing. It was the easiest thing to sell if it could be got out. Mostly, it was pilfered to drink there and then, and security was unbelievable. It was a massive export, and hundreds of thousands of bottles were exported continually from the Yank and Colony

Berths. Lorries would unload in the shed directly into a cage with watchmen present twenty-four hours a day.

When it was to be loaded, a watchman would travel with the bogey driver to the stage end and watch until the crane hoisted it off the quay. There would be a watchman on the deck, sometimes with the ship's boss, the hatch boss, and even the first mate. Two watchmen would be 'down below' watching it being stored, mostly in the lockers, or if it was a big consignment, under the combings or even down the lower hold. At first, every single board would be scrutinised, but as the day wore on, it became tedious and people's attention would wonder; all the time, the dockers would be waiting for the chance while appearing to be plodding away loading it. Eventually, the mate might go to attend to something else or the boss might go for a cup of tea and the dockers would know they were in with a chance, with the minimum number of people seeing to security.

The crane driver would be watching and waiting for someone to lean on the ships rail with his back to the hatch or be in earnest conversation with somebody, and when a window of opportunity appeared in the surveillance, they would all see it at once and the driver would touch a board full of cases of whisky on the deck momentarily and men would appear from nowhere and remove a whole layer in literally seconds. It had to be a whole layer, as one or two cases would be noticed right away. The crane driver would then lift the pallet down below and the rest of the whisky would be stowed without anyone realising that the board was short. The cases would be secreted around the ship, sometimes down other hatches where there were no watchmen or on the deck among the winches and other machinery.

To qualify for a drink or a bottle, dependant on how much had been lifted, you had to touch one of the boxes as it passed through and a man was seen to slap a box as a docker ran along the ship with it in his arms to qualify. Everybody would get a drink who had been involved. It really was a team effort, and sometimes bottles would be passed up to the crane driver or down to men on the quay.

Up to this point, it wasn't apparent that anything had gone missing, but when the sounds of the holdsmen singing down below drifted up, they knew. One ship's boss was seen wringing his hands in despair and shouting, 'How in God's name did they manage to get it? I haven't taken my eyes off it'.

But he had. He just hadn't realised.

The men had nothing. They'd say to each other, 'Go on, lads, 'ave a swig of this. It'll warm ye rup. Good Scotch whisky'.

The consequences of all this free alcohol could be deadly, and there was a story of a man full of whisky falling from the quay into the water unnoticed and because of the state he was in, he drowned.

Another holdsman got so drunk that they had to carry him off the ship and through the shed to get a lorry driver to take him out of the Gladstone gate. If the police saw him going home in that state they would know he'd been at the stolen whisky. The men lifted him on top of the loaded lorry and secured his arms and legs under the ropes.

There was a 'blitz' on the gate, with a dozen policemen searching everybody passing through and the Land Rover jeep ticking over in case someone made a break for it. The lorry driver handed his notes in and drove out of the gate with the man lying there unnoticed and still unconscious. Around the corner in Knowsley Road, the man was lifted down and miraculously seemed to come to, enough to get on a bus to take him home.

It was in the middle of winter and the kids had built a wall of snow about a foot high across the wide back entry near his house. As he swayed up the entry to go in the back door, he tripped over the wall and fell flat on his face and his false teeth shot out, disappearing into the darkness. He was crawling up the back path when his wife came out and saw him.

'Ye drunken get. Fancy comin' home in that state', she remarked.

By way of explanation, he replied, 'Maggie, there was whisky goin' at a Yankee boat. They were all drinkin' it'.

He then mentioned that he'd lost his teeth in the snow and the kids playing in the entry were all lighting matches and looking for them. The teeth were found and handed in at the back door by a young lad who was given a sixpence as a thank you.

Blitz on the Gate

A lot of humour on the docks was created by the need to outwit the police. If there were ships loading suit lengths or whisky, or ships discharging salmon or other expensive items, there would be a blitz on the gate and the searches became more frequent. The police would search everybody, instead of picking people out at random. A bobby would stand with his back to the Yankee Berth and the men would be walking down to go out the Gladstone gate. There'd be a jeep by the gate and the bobbies would be sitting in it.

When the Yankee boats were in, an awful lot of whiskey was loaded. It was one of the biggest exports. One time, because of the thousands of cases of whisky being loaded, and with the added risk of theft, the police had increased security.

It was seven o'clock in the morning, and the men who'd been working nights on a Yankee boat were walking towards the gate. As they approached, they realised that there was a blitz and every single docker was being searched. If they had a bottle of whiskey on them, they'd turn 'round to go back to hide it until security wasn't so tight. Maybe another day, or maybe in the afternoon, or maybe they'd go out the Hornby gate; it was always easier to get out the Hornby gate. The bobby would watch for anyone turning back and he'd grab them and search them.

One docker came walking towards the bobby; he must have known he'd have to get searched, as they were searching everyone. He knew that if he turned back, he's copped, and if he carries on, he's copped. He walked to the gate and the bobby said, 'Right, lad, in the hut'. As the bobby turned, this fella started to run. He ran past the bobby, out the Gladstone gate, and right down Fort road.

The bobby shouted and the other bobbies came piling out of the police hut, jumped in the jeep, and sped off right down Fort road after him.

The fella was going like a steam engine, like a railway train. He got to the bottom and turned right, under the railway bridge. The Police jeep turned right at the traffic lights and up past the Winnie's Pub, this fella was still going like a rocket. The police jeep slowed down and one of the bobbies jumped out and carried on the chase behind the fella. The jeep then accelerated in front of him and the bobbies jumped out and grabbed him. When they searched him, he had nothing on him. They knew he hadn't dumped anything because he had been in sight all the time.

The bobby asked, 'Why have ye ran out the gate when you've got nothin' on ye?'

The fella said, 'I was gonna carry somethin' out tomorra, an' wanted te see if I could beat ye'.

Full House

If you were caught going out of the gate with anything at all you would be sacked immediately. The police would within twenty minutes of you being stopped, arrive at your house to search it. The assumption was that this might be the first time you'd been caught but not be the first time you'd 'carried out'.

A sharp-eyed policeman noticed a dock gateman driving through the gate in his car and heading towards the West Gladstone. These men were employed by the Mersey Docks and Harbour Board to operate the Lock gates and wore a naval type uniform. One would imagine that they'd be beyond reproach. The policeman knew that there wasn't a ship going in or out and waited for him to return. He searched the car as it came back when normally it would be waved through; it was found to contain pilfered cargo in the boot.

The police immediately went to his home and found his garage, garden shed, and even a room in his house full of stolen goods. He hadn't sold or used any of the items. He'd just stolen and stored them. Maybe he got a kick out of getting away with it for so long. The joke went around the docks like wildfire that they had to give a gang of dockers a day and a half loading off to clear the house. Of course, nobody but nobody would suspect a dock gateman. He was fined and lost his job.

Gorilla in the Cask

There was a huge cask in a ship. It was a big barrel with metal bands on it, and it was stored in the 'tween decks. One of the dockers wondered what was in the barrel. He had a little gimlet and screwed it into the barrel, and then turned it and turned it until he'd bored right through the wood. He unscrewed the gimlet and something seeped out. The fella tasted it and said, 'Friggin' 'ell, is tha' whiskey or somethin'?'

He said to the fellas, 'Go an' get ye cups, lads'.

So, all the dockers were standing there, holding their cups out and drinking it, saying, 'Friggin' 'ell, it's firewater, tha', firewater'.

They thought it was whisky.

Over a couple of days, fellas from other hatches got to know there was alcohol, and they were all coming down, taking the stick out of the barrel holding their cups out, and putting the stick back in, and saying 'Firewater, tha'.

The man who came to pick the barrel up found out that most of the alcohol had gone.

One fella piped up, "Ey, mate. They've drank the friggin' lot'.

The man said to them, 'D'ye know what's in it? It's an Ape. It was goin' te one of the universities an' had been preserved in alcohol'.

One Docker said, 'So ye're tellin' us there's a friggin' pickled Gorilla in there an' it's been floatin' in the alcohol, an' all the lads have been drinkin' it for bloody days 'n' days?'

All the dockers were going, 'Argh!'

All in a Dinner Hour

When small transistor radios first became available, one man walked out of the gate with one in every pocket during his lunch hour. He came back and repeated the performance before getting back to work at one o'clock. The talk was that he'd made seventy pounds in one hour and this was at a time when twenty pounds for a week's work would be gasped at.

Frankenstein's Monster

One time, a winch that was out on the open deck of a ship had been burnt out by a gang of dockers. Deckhands would quite often build a small shelter of odd bits of wood and canvas to keep the cold wind off them. They would run the winch with the brake slightly on, which resulted in the friction heating up the winch casing to keep them warm. This sometimes resulted in damage to the machinery.

A couple of engineers were repairing one of the winches, and had taken it to pieces. They had removed the huge copper armature and went for their lunch. While they were gone, one of the dockers, realising how valuable the copper was, went and borrowed an axe from one of the ships.

He chopped the armature in half, and then put two pieces of rope on it like braces. The fella stood inside it and lifted it up, put the ropes over his shoulders and put his coat back on. It was so heavy that he walked stiff legged, like 'Frankenstein's monster', out the dock gate, past the police, and took the copper to the scrap yard. He weighed it in and came flying back and took the other half, and then walked back out the gate and took that to be weighed in before coming back to work at one o'clock.

When the ship repairers returned, they were looking for the armature and couldn't believe it had gone. They knew the weight of it and wondered how it could have disappeared. The two men informed the police that someone had stolen the copper armature out of the winch. The police came and started to look thinking that it must have been dumped somewhere, as they didn't think for one minute that someone could have lifted it. They didn't realise that a fella had actually walked right past them out of the gate with it. The docker who'd taken it sat laughing quietly to himself as he watched all the bobbies buzzing round trying to find it.

Chink in the Armour

Along the line of docks just past the Alexandra Dock was a conveyor belt for sending sugar from the sugar boats out of the dock estate and into silos on the other side of the Dock Road (Tate and Lyles sugar refinery was nearby). It was covered in a corrugated asbestos shed and traffic passed under it as they drove along. The police must have assumed that there was no risk, as nobody would bother to steal unrefined sugar, and there was never any apparent police presence or even an old watchman there.

The conveyor had been running most days for years until somebody decided to make contact with someone working at the silo, and before long, all kinds of cargo was being thrown onto the belt and was recovered on the other side of the Dock Road moments later. People talk, and as soon as it was realised there was a chink in the armour, it was flooded with people wanting a piece of the action. The police soon got to know about it and eventually some men were caught, prosecuted, and sacked.

Inventive Genius

Men could be very inventive. The police stopped a man with a wheelbarrow containing rubbish. The bobby rooted through the rubbish and found nothing hidden, so he let him continue. The man made several more trips that day, each time with a load of rubbish that was duly searched without result. That afternoon, the police got a call from the Colony Berth to inform them to be on the lookout, as somebody had stolen six wheelbarrows.

Me Cabbages

A docker with a small bag of pigeon droppings he'd scraped up to use on his allotment held the bag up as he passed through the gate and called to the police 'fertiliser'. He was ordered to empty the content out onto the cobbles. The docker said, "Ar 'ey, mate. It's only pigeon shite for me cabbages." He then proceeded to empty the contents over the policeman's boots and trousers.

The same police were not averse to taking a couple of half crowns under a baggage pass as ship's crews passed through the gate with a carton or two of cigarettes over their allocation.

Lamb on the Bike

When meat boats started to arrive in the Gladstone Dock, a gang was paid to stand at the gate and unload wagons that the police picked out for special attention. Some drivers knew how to stack lamb carcasses so that an extra line of them could be stacked without the length of the load being increased. The offal was stored in the cavity of the animal and it was easy to add extra offal among the load.

The police paid most attention to the vehicles because of the size of the lambs, and one docker noticed that men were rarely searched when this commodity was being discharged. He had a motorbike and jammed a whole lamb onto the seat behind him, with his overcoat on it, buttoned up, and with his cap on the top. He bent the two front legs over his shoulders and rode through the Gladstone gate with his pillion passenger attracting only a cursory glance from the bobby talking to someone by the police hut. The fella got home and cut the lamb up with a joiner's saw on the kitchen floor. Some of the neighbours were treated to large joints of meat that evening.

Guts on the Bike

At the meat berth, a fella seized an opportunity to carry out. He took all the offal – the heart, kidneys, liver, and so forth – from inside a sheep's carcass, he then stuffed the whole lot down his shirt and put his coat on.

The fella was riding out the dock gate on his bike when he saw a bobby. In a panic, he started riding faster to get out of the way before the bobby clocked him, but he ran into the railway lines on the quay and flew right over the handlebars of his bike and fell flat on his face. He didn't half take a fall. The bobby saw him fall and ran out of the hut, and rolled him over. As he turned him, the fella's shirt burst open and all the offal spilt out and oozed onto the road. The bobby thought it was the fella's intestines and fainted. The fella sat up, got himself together, stuffed all the offal back in his shirt, and ran out the gate with his bike before the other policemen realised that anything was amiss. And there's the bobby, lying on the floor out cold; he'd fainted with the shock.

Away on a Bike

A lot of bikes were exported from the docks. The bikes would be packed in boxes in separate pieces, ready to be assembled, as they could be transported more easily. Men would steal all the parts and assemble them. They'd just tighten everything up and blow the tyres up. The bikes would be shiny because they were brand new, so dockers would go and scrape some muck up from out between the railway lines and splatter the bike with it and then ride out of the gate on it.

When they got home, they'd put the hosepipe on the bike to clean it and make it look brand new again. Dockers would come back and steal another one. With all the bikes that were going missing, it's amazing that nobody rumbled it.

Disappearing Dinner

Americans celebrate Thanksgiving with a traditional meal of roast turkey. A big black guy was the cook on a Yankee boat, and he had cooked a huge turkey for the crew. The galley had windows that looked out onto a passageway between the cooking area and the ship's rail. There were also bars on the windows. The cook had left the windows open and locked the door while this monster of a turkey was in the middle of the galley on the table where it had just come out of the oven and left to cool. The smell was magnificent and soon attracted the attention of several dockers, who could see this prize through the bars but couldn't reach it.

After some thought, it was decided that a couple of them should go over to the China Berth to try and find a piece of bamboo or something similar, and someone returned from this foray with a piece of bamboo about twelve feet long. They sharpened the end with a penknife and slid it through the bars toward the turkey on the table, and stabbed it just enough to secure it.

Three pairs of hands then lifted the bird off the table and drew it towards the window and up to the bars. A couple of men kept watch, as the cook could return at any minute. It was a delicate operation and the bamboo pole they were using bent like a fishing rod under the weight. Slowly but surely the prize was inched towards them until it was up against the bars. One docker got his fingers through the bars and others joined in until the turkey was pulled through the grill in pieces and consumed on the spot by a laughing gang. The bamboo pole was thrown over the side into the dock and they dispersed.

When the cook returned later, he saw the empty table and there was absolute uproar that the crew's dinner had disappeared. Someone said later that he was overheard insisting to the mate that someone had a duplicate key to the galley, and yes, he was certain that he had locked up when he left. They couldn't imagine what had really happened. They actually called the police, who couldn't figure it out either, but the dockers knew.

Chicken Scoff

Another time a docker took a huge tin that had six cooked chickens in it and opened the tin with his penknife. He put a newspaper on the floor like a plate and slid the chickens out onto the paper. The next minute, all the dockers gathered round.

'Go on, lads, get stuck in', he invited.

Dockers were sitting 'round the newspaper scoffing all the chickens; the food was always good at the Yank.

Fruit Cocktail

Some fellas were called 'Galley Rats'. When ships came in, especially passenger ships, they carried a small amount of goods, but mainly it would be the passengers' luggage. As soon as the ship had docked, certain fellas would hang around the galley all the time. The Yankee boats would bring in fabulous food. When the Yankee food came in it wasn't secure. It was piecemeal and cardboard cases containing large tins that could be easily opened.

On one particular occasion, a docker was down a Yankee boat and there were great big catering tins of fruit cocktail. The fella opened a whole tin weighing about fifteen pounds. He was just picking at it. He couldn't possibly eat it. The

Yankee mate came down the ladder behind him and copped him.

'Are you hungry, mister?' he asked him.

'Er, yeah', he replied.

'You better be', the mate said. 'Because you will eat every bit of that or I'll pick up the phone and have the police from the gate here in a minute'.

The fella couldn't hide because he was working on the ship and his number was in. If he ran away or hid, they would say, 'Give us all the numbers of all the men down below'. Fellas could be caught easily.

The Yankee mate shouted to one of the crew to go and get a big spoon from the galley. The crewman came back with the spoon. The Mate handed the spoon to the fella and said, 'Now you will eat ever bit of that'.

The docker sat there with this big tin. It was like a bucket.

'Go on', the mate continued.

'I can't eat it all', the fella said.

'Well, you should have thought of that before you opened it', the mate said.

All the other dockers gathered around, and the mate was standing there looking very determined.

'D'ye wanna bit, lads', the fella asked.

'Nah, ye all right', they answered.

He was starting to force it down and said to the mate, 'Is tha' enough?'

'No! You'll eat every bit of that', the mate insisted.

The fella was forcing the fruit cocktail down and suddenly he ran up the ladder and vomited over the ship's rail.

The mate came up after him and said, 'Now let that be a lesson to you'.

Tongue 'n' Boots

One time, The Hen opened a big tin of tongue with his penknife. He ate the gelatine out of it and then threw the tin over the side of the ship.

Someone saw him and told him, 'Ye know there's kids in the world friggin' starvin'. You need drowin' for doin' tha', you, ye bastard'.

It went round the dock like wild fire.

Someone said, 'Ye know The Hen? He opened a friggin' bit tin of tongue, ate the jelly, and threw the friggin' tongue in the dock. Ar, for Christ's sake'.

The dockers were appalled at the wastage.

The same fella at the China Berth had stolen a pair of 'Tuff' boots coming in from Malaysia. The next day, he stole another pair that were a day younger and threw the other boots in the dock.

Someone else said, 'You want throwin' in the dock ye friggin' self, you'.

Dockers' Uniform

At the China Berth, a lot of Keynote brand stuff for Littlewoods came ashore. One time, checked shirts, white trousers, and tuff boots were in abundance, so loads of dockers just helped themselves. Because of the pilfering, you'd see everyone who'd been working at the China wearing the cargo. All the dockers were dressed the same. The funny thing was that no one rumbled it. You'd think the police would go, 'Hang on, what's the cargo here', but they didn't. It was because of scenes like this that dockers referred to the police as 'Pantomime Bobbies'.

Dockers would pilfer things such as coffee and cakes. They'd pass the word around and say, 'There's coffee goin' at number three hatch, chocolate cake goin' at number one hatch, an' apple pie at number four'.

Men lost their jobs for silly things like taking oranges, apples, and stuff like that.

Apple Sammy

Apple Sammy had bad feet. He wore surgical boots of very soft leather that were always brightly polished, and he walked with his feet splayed out – not ten to two, but more a quarter to three. When he rode his bike, his feet stuck out and he pedalled with his heels. When he walked, he had a rolling motion from side to side.

A fruit boat was discharging at the Yankee Berth, and as usual, a case of apples was opened so the dockers could help themselves. This was to prevent dozens of cases being broached and was accepted practice. It was, however, still illegal to take anything out of the dock gate, and it was immediate dismissal if anyone was caught.

Sammy in his gabardine mac, wearing his cap, decided to take the chance. He'd never carried out before, and the police had relaxed security at the gate, as there was nothing being loaded or discharged that day that would attract people to such behaviour.

Sammy stuffed his pockets with apples from the opened case, buttoned his mac up, and rode his bike towards the gate. As bad luck would have it, a lorry driver was just pulling away from the policeman on the gate, having just handed his notes in. The policeman noticed Sammy riding towards him with his coat fastened up to the neck on what was a mild day. He motioned Sammy to go up to the door of the police hut. Sammy knew that he would be searched and that would be that. In a blind panic, he rode through the gate to escape and went down Fort Road like a rocket. The policeman realised that he couldn't catch him and ran back to the door of the police box shouting so that they could get after him in the jeep that was nearly always parked there. By the time the other policemen had jumped in the jeep, Sammy was nearly at the bottom of the road going like an Olympic cyclist, with his feet stuck out like little aeroplane wings.

Horror of horrors, he saw that the traffic lights were on red for him but decided in a flash to go for it and in his fear pedalled even harder going through against the lights like a comet. Unfortunately, a Ribble Bus coming from Crosby was going through the lights at the same time and Sammy flashed across the front of the bus in the blink of an eye and nearly made it into Seaforth Road, but not quite. The bus just caught the back tyre of his bike and spun Sammy and the bike like a propeller. Sammy landed on the pavement and his bike was thrown in the air, it hit the wall, and landed next to him with a crash.

Incredibly, and probably because of the adrenaline rush, he was on his feet in a flash running down Seaforth Road with his feet splayed out in his distinctive rolling motion with apples falling from under his coat and rolling into the road. He came to a street and turned into it, and halfway down turned into another entry that crossed it. Too late! He realised that it was a dead end.

His breath was coming in short struggling gasps, and when he tried the back gate at the end and found it locked, he realised that he didn't have the strength to climb over the wall and huddled in the corner, resigning himself to his fate. Through the sweat running down his face and into his eyes, he saw the dark blue mackintosh and peaked cap of the man walking towards him with what looked like a notebook in one hand and a pencil in the other.

'Okay, mate', said Sammy. 'I can't run anymore. It was only a few apples. I'm turnin' me self in (Gasp). You'll get no trouble from me'.

The man looked confused and turned and rattled the latch of the door next to where Sammy was cowering in surrender.

'I don't know what you mean, mate', he said. 'I'm the Gas Man and I'm out reading meters'.

Chapter 6
Those Silly Things Young Men Do

Racing Bogies

A gang of dockers took some electric bogies. They were small trucks and very, very heavy, full of massive batteries. The lads were racing the bogies towards the edge of the lock and pushing the handle down and the bogey would turn and just miss the edge. But anyone steering it actually went over the edge of the lock though the bogey didn't. The dockers were all seeing who could get the closest to the edge. What they were doing was dangerous. They could have been killed. They could have gone into the dock.

All the gang were taking it in turn, one fella charged towards the lock and pushed the handle down. He would have made it, but he got frightened and jumped off. With the momentum of the bogey going forward, the steering straightened up and it went right over the edge and fell in to the water.

The dock was about fifty feet deep, but where the ships came in over the lock it wasn't as deep. There was a concrete ledge and some of the ships only just got over it. With the bogey going over and in the dock, and landing on the ledge under the water, they couldn't get any ships in or out. A diver was sent down to hook the bogey up and lift it out. All those involved were sacked. The whole lot were cleared out.

The Kremlin

Box three, or number three pen was so full of communist sympathisers it was known by the dockers as 'The Kremlin'. It was the Huskisson Dock area, further down the line from the Gladstone, and cars were loaded there from time to time.

The procedure on the quay was to push the cars from where they were stored towards the stage end by the designated hatch, onto a steel framework that would allow the crane to lift them down below. There were two sets of plates that the car was pushed onto, and these coincided with the wheels on the car. When the crane heaved, the plates would tilt either side of the tyres into a 'V' shape so it couldn't roll out of the jig. One man would steer the car through the open window while the others pushed from behind, and the car was supposed to be rolled right up to the plates and carefully and slowly pushed on top of the metal plates in the last few inches.

A crowd of young dockers had been working at this for a few hours and the hatch was filling with Morris Minors. As boredom set in, they started to act the goat and were pushing like mad while the guy steering through the window struggled to turn the wheel fast enough to line the cars up with the lifting jig.

Eventually the inevitable happened. They were pushing like mad and the car got a fair bit of speed up. The man steering was protesting that they were pushing too hard and he struggled to turn it through the gate. Too late, they realised they had to stop it going any further and instead of pushing were now pulling on the back bumper to stop it going out of the other side, which it did. It ran into the side of the ship, and the two front wheels dropped off the edge of the quay with the front bumper hard up against the ship's side and there it stayed.

For a moment, maybe because of the car hitting the ship, the ship moved out ever so slightly and the nose of the car slid down a bit further and the rear wheels started to lift off the floor. The ship moved back again and there was a crunching noise as it squashed the front of the bonnet.

The ship moved out again, and again the car slipped further down into the gap, lifting the back of the car even further into the air. Men watched fascinated, as it appeared the ship had a mind of its own, and was eating the car slowly and deliberately. There was a bang as the windscreen shattered and the car was now nearly vertical, its underside clearly visible. The car was inching down faster towards the water as more and more of it was flattened. The dockers who'd been pushing it were shocked by what was happening, and the person doing the steering was adamant it wasn't his fault.

'It's not my fault. You were all acting the twat. I couldn't reach the fuckin' 'and brake', he insisted.

The ship's boss came stumbling down the gangway in disbelief and came over to where the empty jig was. 'Fuckin' 'ell', was all he could say. 'Fuckin' 'ell'.

They watched as the ship moved out slightly and the Morris Minor disappeared from view. A split second later, they heard a splash, and a plume of water erupted between the side of the ship and the quay. The glass from the windscreen scattered on the quay, the only sign that the car had been there.

All this had drawn a crowd, and the lads pushing the car disappeared, knowing quite well what would happen to them. The only one remaining was the fella who'd been steering who was repeating to the boss, 'I couldn't reach the 'and brake. Don't be lookin' at me'.

Super Wellies

'Married gear' was a term used to describe a system of lifting using the ship's own winches. A derrick was positioned over the quay (the yard arm) with another over the hatch of the ship (the up and down). The cables were directed from their respective winches up through gin blocks attached to the end of the derricks, and both cables were joined together by a shackle with a hook attached, hence the name 'married gear'. By one deckhand working the winch to heave or lower and his opposite number doing the same, the hook could be lifted out of the hold across the deck of the ship and lowered to the quay with slings of cargo.

A deckhand from the Gladstone Dock was employed to 'Pass the word'. This was when men were working out of sight of the men working the winches and they would be directed by hand signals or shouts by somebody who could see for them.

Cargo had been coming ashore all day, and had been lowered to the quay by the deckhand on the yard arm. He lifted the empty hook up for the man on the up and down to pull across to the hatch, and as he then started lowering to allow some slack, he misjudged and lowered too much. Instead of the hook pulling across above head height, it travelled about three feet above the deck.

The man passing the word wore a thick leather belt as did most dockers, and by a million to one chance, it caught under his belt. The driver on the yard arm realised his mistake and heaved to lift the hook up without realising the man was caught up. This lifted the man off his feet and fifteen feet up in the air. The sudden force pulled the man out of his wellies, which stood upright on the deck. He was unhurt and his belt had held. He was lowered gently to the deck amid nervous laughter from him and those who'd witnessed the near miss. Immediately, he was nicknamed superman, but soon after it was changed to 'Super Wellies'.

Wallop

One time at the Hornby Dock, a rat ran along the tween decks. A docker saw it and threw a piece of timber at it and managed to hit it. The rat fell out of the tween deck and into the lower hold.

A fella called Sid was working down below. He had a couple of buttons undone on his shirt and the rat just happened to fall down his shirt. It was a complete fluke. The first thing he did was grab his shirt. The rat could be seen running around inside it.

His mate, in a screaming panic, picked a piece of wood up and started to wallop the rat with it – Bang! Bang! Bang – as hard as he could, forgetting that it was inside Sid's shirt. Sid fell to the floor moaning in agony but the fella gave the rat another belt before he realised what he was doing. They had to get a box down and take poor Sid to hospital, as he could hardly breathe. He was kept in all night with badly bruised ribs and he was strapped up for a fortnight.

Chapter 7
Posh Bob

Bob was a real character; he was always doing mad and crazy things. Sometimes without his realizing it, they were actually quite dangerous. He was a practical joker and well known for being wild. Nineteen years old, he stood six feet tall with a slim frame topped off with curly hair. He had a long thin nose, and a twinkle was always in his eye. Bob had developed this posh accent. He spoke like a BBC announcer and he came from Bootle. His voice always attracted curious looks among the working class people from there.

When Bob first started work at the docks, you'd see fellas looking over the deck of the ship at Bob with this posh voice. Bob, in his upper crust accent, would say things like, 'Heave a bit, driver', or 'Right, lads. Go and get your tango', and it sounded hysterical.

Rip

Bob was always playing practical jokes. He'd just rip the pocket off your coat and you'd see a nice clean piece of material against the rest that had been faded by the sun. His friend Tony had a Yankee army jacket, khaki coloured and blanket lined. As Bob walked away from Tony one day, he pulled at Tony's pocket and ripped his coat right under the arm and a big flap of fabric fell down by his knee. As he walked 'round, you could just see the blanket lining.

Bob was screaming laughing and appalled by what he'd done. 'Tony, I'm sorry. I didn't realise. I'm sorry. I'm sorry', he said as he was running away laughing. All the other lads thought it was hysterical and were laughing.

"Ay, Bob, you've ripped all the side of me coat off', Tony said. So for days after that when Bob saw Tony he was always ready for flight, with his foot pointing in the direction he was going to run. When Bob was talking to Tony, he'd put his hands on the side of his pockets in case Tony went to snatch his pockets off. Tony left it for about four or five days and just pretended he'd forgotten about it.

One day, they were both standing by the Yankee Berth, which was near the Graving Dock, (the dry dock in the Gladstone Dock). Bob must have forgotten, or he must have thought Tony had forgotten, and quick as a flash, Tony ripped Bob's top pocket and it came off.

Bob said, "Ar, me mother will sew that back on'. Tony threw the pocket and it went down the dry dock. There was no water in the dry dock, but there were always pools of water, and it was about fifty feet down. Bob said, 'It's bad enough ripping my pocket, but you've actually thrown it down the dry dock'. Tony just replied with, 'Argh, balls on it'.

Nailed It

After Bob ripped the pocket off Tony's coat, and Tony had already ripped the pocket off Bob's coat, they were working down below on a Yankee boat and there were some pieces of timber. Bob left his coat on top of the timber. Some fellas were working down below, and Tony borrowed a hammer and some six-inch nails. He took Bob's coat, opened it, and nailed it to a piece of timber. He folded the coat over so you couldn't see the nails.

It came to dinner time. 'Ge' rup out of it'. There was a big scramble up the ladder, where every minute's precious. Bob was the last. He grabbed his coat, but as he went to run, he was pulled up with a jerk. When he opened his coat, he said, 'Argh, friggin' hell. I wouldn't have minded, but you've bent the nails over'. All the lads were laughing like mad, and Bob was laughing himself.

He was seen later walking down the quay with this plank across his shoulders, wearing his coat still nailed to it, to roars of laughter from the men on the quay.

Little Tiny Tie

Bob started to come into work with a little pair of scissors, and there were dockers who'd wear ties. Manual labourers who had dirty old caps on would have a tie on. Bob would be talking to them and he'd just cut their tie off, leaving the knot with a little short piece of tie. You'd see a load of dockers all walking round wearing these little tiny ties. It was like something in a comedy show.

Smoke 'n' Teeth

One morning in the Fort Cafe, everyone was sitting down eating bacon butties and drinking cups of tea. The next minute, Bob turned up on his motorbike. He backed it into the cafe with the engine running, and then closed the choke and he revved it up. A big cloud of smoke wafted in the canteen. All the dockers were running out, choking and coughing. Some of the old fellas were coughing so much that their false teeth came out. Bob put the bike in gear and sped away. He was screeching with laughter. All the dockers were shouting after him, "Ey, ye mad bastard, ye'.

Dempsey's Tea

One afternoon, Dempsey was sitting in the Fort Cafe holding a newspaper with his glasses on reading. Bob came in looking for what depredation he could do. He had a mug of tea and said in his BBC announcers voice, 'Hello, John'. Dempsey said, 'Alright, Bob'.

Dempsey had the paper outstretched in front of him and Bob just came up and poured the whole pint of tea down the front of the paper. Dempsey just kept reading. He didn't even blink. He just pretended nothing had happened. The tea ran down the paper, off the table, and all over the front of his trousers. The paper started to fall to pieces. Dempsey licked his fingers and peeled one of the pages over so he could read the other side.

The whole place was up laughing. It was the fact that Dempsey didn't react. Bob ran out and kept looking at Dempsey. He'd go near him and he'd scoot away, like a kid would. Dempsey was one of the boys and took it in good sport.

Little Coconut Cake

Another time in the Fort cafe, a glass case was on the counter and Bob realised there was no base in it. It was just free standing and there were little coconut cakes in it. When he thought the woman wasn't looking, Bob pulled on the glass case. As he pulled on it further, it overlapped the counter and a cake fell out. He pushed the glass case back and put the cake in his pocket.

Bob went outside, broke it up, and fed it to the pigeons. The woman had seen him take the cake but turned a blind eye until she saw what he was up to outside. She came out and said, 'Well, I wouldn't friggin' mind if ye was 'ungry, ye friggin' robbin' bastard, ye'. Bob had a big red face. He put his hands up and said, 'Ay', laughing.

Old Carter

The Red Hut canteen was just inside the Gladstone Gate on the left. It was painted red, with a roof covered in roofing felt. It was always full, being the nearest place for a cup of tea to dockers at the Yank, Colony Berth, C.P.R., or even the China. Bob and Tony pushed through the door, out of the rain, and looked for a place to sit. They were working at the Yank and had come in for their dinner.

The place was full of dockers drinking mugs of tea, eating or smoking. There was a sprinkling of other people who worked on the docks – lorry drivers, engineers, and the like. The two lads picked a place to sit and Tony went to get a couple of bowls of soup. Bob busied himself with the tin opener on a penknife he had with him. When Tony came back, Bob took some stewed steak from the tin he'd just opened and let it sink into the hot oxtail soup, and then waited for it to warm up the meat.

Tony sat down and noticed that they were facing an old carter, whose horse and cart they'd passed on the way in. He was an elderly man who wore an old sack, split up the side, and tied with a piece of string around the middle. His head was covered by one of the corners, which made it stick up like a pixie hood. He also had a bowl of soup and sipped it carefully, relishing the heat.

Tony was sipping his soup and noticed that Bob had become unusually quiet. He wondered what he was up to. There was always something! Bob dipped into the soup and lifted a piece of meat out on his spoon, making a slightly exaggerated slurp as he ate it. The old carter glanced toward him and looked away again. Bob fished about and got another piece of the meat ready. When the old man met Bob's gaze for a second time, Bob gave a loud slurp for effect, and ate the chunk of meat. This time it hadn't gone unnoticed and the old man started to search around for the chunks of meat he imagined must be in his soup.

Bob prepared the 'Coup de grace'. He found the biggest chunk of steak he could and spoke as he slurped the spoonful into his mouth, talking and chewing.

'What's the matter, Pop. No meat in your soup?' he asked.

'No, no', said the old carter, agitated as he started to scoop the spoon into the bowl, searching.

'They're taking liberties with you', advised Bob. 'They try it on with everyone'.

The old man got up and went back to the counter with the remains of his soup. Bob and Tony were trying hard to suppress their laughter and others nearby were paying attention after hearing some of the conversation.

"Ey, luv. Dees no meet in me soop', he said.

'It's just soup. Oxtail soup. There's no meat in', replied the woman.

'Yis, dee is. Dig down te the bottom of de pot'.

'I've just told you. It's oxtail soup', she repeated.

The old man was now losing it and raised his voice, oblivious to the laughter now beginning to swell up around the canteen.

'It's alright for ye, Blue Eyes, isn't it? Big chunks of meat an' tha".

The woman was now frustrated and from Bootle stock who didn't suffer fools gladly.

'Sling yer 'ook, ye soft old get'.

'Don't call me a soft owl get, ye fuckin' scrubber', he shouted as he leaned over the counter and lashed the remains of the soup at her.

This scenario now had everybody's attention, and when the woman picked up a huge jug of milk and threw it over him, the crowd was almost ready for it and those nearest turned their backs before it caught the carter in the face and spattered everyone nearby. The old guy was a sight; he still had the sack on with the string tied around his waist with the pixie hood sticking up, and now the milk was running down his front.

'I'll get the police. Just fuck off ... with ye horse,' the woman added as an afterthought.

Bob and Tony slid out of the door and ran toward the Yankee Berth but not before seeing the old guy, as a last statement, smashing his fist down on a tray of cream cakes on the counter, further spattering everybody within range. They stood just inside the shed laughing fit to die and watched until the old carter emerged shouting and waving his arms.

He heaved himself up onto the cart full of wooden cases, slapped the horse on its rear quarters with the reins, and trundled out of the Gladstone gate over the cobbles, his pixie hood just visible over the boxes. Bob and Tony both waited until he was almost at the bottom by the Caradoc Pub before they emerged, still with tears of laughter running down their faces.

Heave a Bit, Driver

Bob was working on a Yankee boat, and there was lots of really expensive paper that was wrapped in very, very thick brown paper. The bales were about the size of an armchair and were quite heavy. Bob placed a sling around the bales of paper and in his posh voice said to the crane driver, 'Lower a bit, drive'. He took the hook and said, 'Lower a bit more'. The driver let a bit more slack off, and then a bit more, and shouted, 'What 'av ye got there?'

Bob said, 'Just lower away, driver'. Bob threaded the hook under some odd bits of timber. He then hooked it on to the sling of paper and shouted, 'Get out the way, lads'. Bob said to the crane driver, 'Go ahead, driver. Heave a bit'. So the driver heaved. Well, of course, threading it was like putting something under a floorboard. As the crane started to heave, all the timber was going bang, bang, ba bang, bang, bang. It was shattering and the timber was breaking. The driver was saying, 'What 'av ye got there?'

Bob shouted, 'You've got nothing. Heave a bit more. You've got nothing'.

The driver didn't realise and said, 'What 'av ye got there? The friggin' back wheels of the crane are liftin' off the railway line on the roof'. He could feel the crane lifting and someone said, "Ey, Bob. Ye know wha' I mean. There's a fella heavin' away and he doesn't know what he's got on the end of this'.

Bob just couldn't stop laughing and laughing. Common sense prevailed and the fall was removed from under the timber.

Scatter the Muster

One day Bob nearly killed himself. All the dockers (the muster) were standing there waiting to book on. Fellas would wear old army coats and stuff like that. Their wives might get them an army coat or a great coat, from the army and navy' stores. You would see fellas even on a hot day wearing overcoats and caps, as it could be quite cold down the docks.

All the muster was filing past and a fella was calling, 'Down below. On the deck. On the quay'.

The next minute, Bob came screaming up with his motorbike, blowing the horn – beep, be beep, beep, beeeeeeep! 'Get out the way, lads', he shouted, and he went to scatter the muster. All of a sudden, the front wheel of the motorbike hit one of the railway lines that ran at the back and at the front of the dock sheds. Bob hit one of the little junctions that cocked the front wheel and it jammed. He went right up in the air and over the crowd and smacked down on the cobbles. Some of the dockers thought he'd killed himself. A couple of days later, Bob came back to work with a great big scab on the end of his nose. One docker said, 'Tha' young Bob. The mad get. He could 'av bloody killed himself. He didn't 'arv fall.'

Bag of Shite Flour

Where the ships came in through the lock there was quite a flat area. The dock sheds didn't run right down to the lock. Near the lock there was a big concrete apron. It was like a car park. One day, a gang of young dockers were there playing football in their dinner hour.

Bob disappeared into the shed and a minute later he came out with a rope sling over his shoulder and a two-wheel truck. On it was a big bag of what they used to call 'shite flour'. It wasn't pure white; it was more grey. The bags were really heavy, weighing a hundredweight and a half, and very loosely stitched so you'd get covered in it. Bob attached them both to the sling.

At the China Berth the cranes were on top of the roof and they ran on railway lines. Some cranes were also on the quay'. The crane driver wondered what was going on but wasn't too concerned. He lowered the fall down to Bob, and Bob slung the flour and the truck up and shouted for him to put it on the roof.

By the time it was lifted up, Bob had reached the top of the stairs and had come out of the door at the top. He unhooked it again and then wheeled it right along the roof to the end where the ships came in through the lock. Bob shouted down to the fellas, 'Hey, lads, get out of the way', so they cleared away from the shed to see what he was going to do. They didn't have long to wait.

It was fifty feet down to the concrete from the roof and they could see him lifting something on to the low parapet. The next minute, he manhandled the bag of flour and threw it right off the top of the China Berth. When it hit the concrete, it went off like an atom bomb. It went 'bunffff' and formed a huge mushroom cloud.

All the lads were covered in flour and were screaming, laughing, and shouting, "Ey, ye mad bastard'. Bob saw the carnage and thought it was hysterically funny. Everyone could hear Bob howling with laughter. He stood on the roof and shouted down to the lads, 'Hey, lads, what do you think?' The dockers all scattered with the football in case they got the blame.

Purple Dopes

Bob and Tony were in the China loft one day and there were big tins of purple ink for marking the bales of rubber. Bob had one of them full to the brim with a paintbrush. There were some columns painted white. Bob wrote on one 'Tony is a dope'. Tony got the tin and brush and crossed out the name Tony and wrote above it, 'Bob'. So, Bob did the same and crossed out Bob and wrote 'Tony'.

This continued right up the column 'til they could hardly reach anymore, but Tony was determined to win and he had the pot of ink in his left hand. He was on his tiptoes with the brush held right at its very tip between his thumb and forefinger. He was really straining to cross out his name and write in Bob's.

Bob decided he was bored with all this and slapped his hand upward, striking the tin of ink on the bottom with great force. The ink splattered everywhere, all over the both of them – clothes, hair, and faces. The two of them were covered in it and screeching with laughter. Tony even had purple teeth. They had to go down into the avenue where there was a tap and try and wash some of it off. Tony had to put his shoulder right under the tap and all you could see was purple dye running down the gutter. It was crazy!

Kick Start

Bob came into work one morning and looked a bit flustered. He'd come out of his house to go through the King's Park to get the bus and it was drizzling. Bob crossed over Hawthorne Road and was just entering the park when it started to pour with rain, so he started to run with his coat over his head. He was half way through the park when the rain got even heavier and he could just make out a bus nearing the stop in the distance so he put a spurt on. There he was, running like the clappers down the path, holding his coat over his head with one hand, with the rain hitting him in the face.

All he could see was the ground in front of him when suddenly he made out a fat old man right in front of him on two sticks taking up the whole width of the path. Bob was right on top of him and all in a split second. He tried to stop but his foot slipped on the tar, and as he slid to the floor, his other foot came up and kicked the old fella right up the arse and the two of them were in bulk on the path. Bob got up in a flash and jumped over him, shouting, 'Sorry. Sorry', and carried on so he wouldn't miss the bus, leaving the poor old fella flat on his back.

Drum Beats 'n' Barrels

Bob and Tony, apart from being dockers, were both drummers and played in groups. One time, they were at the Yankee Berth working nights. Specialist greases and oils were delivered to the ships. There were some empty fifty-gallon oil drums in the avenue at the Yankee Berth and Bob was going round and hitting them. You could hear them going, 'dong, dong'. He moved the drums around so he knew which tone was what. Tony was walking to the shed and could hear 'dung, ka ka, dung, ka ka, dung, ka, dung dung', and Bob was in the middle of these drums.

A big gang of dockers soon gathered around him. It was like a Hollywood musical. He had two bits of wood and all they could hear were drum beats and a big drum solo.

All the dockers were saying, 'Ay, ay, lad, y'id make a few bob doin' tha'. Ay, ay, listen te this lad playin' the drums. Go 'ed there. Ye could make a few bob doin' that'.

The next minute Tony joined in on some other drums and started playing a basic drum pattern with Bob playing the other beats. All the dockers thought they were fantastic and were saying, 'Go 'ed there, lads. Friggin' brilliant tha', lads. Y'id make a few bob outta tha'.

Disappearing Drummer

Saturday night, Bob was playing the drums with the Silhouettes on Saint Monica's. The same night, he had to be at the docks for eleven o'clock, as he'd been hired to work nights at the Yankee Berth, which included working a 'nugget' . It was big money – almost a week's wages for working a Saturday night. It got to twenty past ten and the group finished one song and announced another one. When they kicked off there were no drums. When they turned around, Bob had disappeared, just like that. He just got off. He wasn't going to miss the nugget for anybody.

Chapter 8
Super Docker

Save Me Brushes

It can be imagined that from time to time things would fall in the dock and they did. Nets called 'save alls' were draped from the ships to the quay to catch any cargo that might fall out of a sling. Even so, there were times when cargo, machinery, or even men fell in.

Ships were sometimes painted when in port, and the painters used long poles with rollers to do the side of the ship at the quayside. On the other side of the ship, either crewmen were lowered in bosun's chairs to chip the old paint off and repaint, or contractors would do it, and a floating platform was sometimes used with different levels connected by ladders for access.

These platforms had a rail all around them to protect the painters.

Even so, at the CPR Berth (Canadian Pacific Railways) one of the painters managed to over reach and fall in. He was wearing an overcoat over his painter's overalls and it weighed him down. He fought his way to the surface as his mates ran down the ladders to the bottom level to reach him. He went under for a second time as they got there and again pushed to the surface against the weight of his sodden clothes.

He was close to the platform and one painter lay down while others held his legs and allowed him to reach out and grab the drowning man's collar. He was pulled out of the water, safely back onto the platform to everybody's relief, and the men began to take off the wet overcoat and overalls.

The man who'd pulled him out asked, 'When ye were gaspin' for air, ye were tryin' te shout somethin', an' when I grabbed ye collar as ye were goin' back under the water, you were still tryin' te shout te me. Wha' was it you were tryin' te say?'

The rescued painter who was drenched through and was shivering replied, 'I was shoutin' for ye te save me brushes cos they're brand new ones'.

Dog in the Dock

On another occasion, a dog had fallen into the dock and couldn't find a way out. There were two sets of steps at the bottom of this dock, one on the China Berth side and one on the CPR side. The poor dog was tired out and had been swimming about for half an hour and was now heading toward the basin where the ships came in through the lock. The only steps there, even if it could recognise them as an escape route, were at the bottom of the west side, and they were a couple of hundred yards away.

The Mammoth floating crane was berthed alongside the CPR quay, and as crowds of men were finishing work, they lined the quays on both sides to watch. Suddenly, one of the crew from the Mammoth stripped down to his underpants and dived in. He started to swim toward the dog, which was frightened and started to swim over to the China side away from him but still towards the huge Gladstone Dock basin, and almost certain drowning.

The lad was a magnificent swimmer, and he turned away from the dog and swam up towards the basin nearer to the CPR side of the dock and out into the wide expanse and round back down in a semi circle to face the animal. He shouted and splashed to frighten the dog into turning around, which it did, and the long journey for the poor thing began as it started back down toward the steps at the far end. The young man kept just far enough away to frighten it into keeping in the right direction and swam to the left or the right as it tried to turn back until at last it saw the dockers at the far end. The dog approached the steps and the crewman swam over to the floating crane and was pulled up by his mates.

Some flotsam and jetsam had been blown into that corner of the dock and the dog couldn't get through it to the steps. The quays were lined with people watching, and the man at the very bottom of the steps realised that the dog was terrified and had no strength left at all, so he shouted, 'Step back, lads'. Like a brigade of guards on parade, all the people took a step back so the dog couldn't see them from the water.

The man at the bottom of the steps agitated the water to move some of the floating debris out of the way and miraculously a small gap of clear water emerged. The dog saw this, and was on his very last dregs of energy, and aimed for the steps and the hand waiting to grab his collar. The man at the steps held on to another man's hand and stretched out as far as he dared.

The last few yards were when they thought they might lose the dog in fifty feet of water, as his eyes seemed to glaze over and he couldn't keep his nose above the surface anymore. All his energy had gone, and suddenly the man who'd been talking to him gently all the time managed to hook a finger in his collar and pull him closer and then change his grip and get a firm grasp. He brought the dog into the steps and heaved him out to a huge cheer around the whole dock.

The lad on the Mammoth who'd gone into the water was standing watching with his chest heaving, with a large towel around him and he waved to the crowd. A round of genuine applause rang out for this young man who'd done such a good deed for this poor, old mongrel dog. It was a full three minutes before the dog could even shake himself, and when he did, there was a scatter of dockers getting away from the spray with false cries of derision. Somebody took the dog over to one of the sheds to let him recover in the warmth. It was suggested that someone write in to the *Liverpool Echo*, but nobody ever did.

Chapter 'n' Verse

It was bad enough 'getting it worked up, ye', but sometimes it was unmerciful. At the China, you could get bales of rubber put in the tanks at the Bow of the ship. They usually put latex rubber in there, which was pumped ashore, but now and again they would put the bales down there.

It was steaming hot, there wasn't much room and it wasn't a proper hatch. It had a lid on it and the crew would unscrew dozens of nuts to get the lid off. No one was sure if they could turn the heating pipes off or if they just didn't bother, but just imagine how hot it got on a warm day. Fellas would be covered in the French chalk that was used to stop the rubber sticking together and you could see the lines of sweat running down their faces. You'd have to work an hour about, as there wasn't much room, and when the hour was up, they'd come climbing out of the tank and say, "Ee y'ar, lads. It's your turn'. A fella once said, "Ang on. There's a minute te go yet'. Can you imagine arguing over sixty seconds? That's how bad it could be. It's no wonder everybody used to run when the China boss walked out in the pen.

One docker asked a young lad if he could go to the Irish Club for a swift half, and said that he would come back at four o'clock and the lad could go home. The trouble was that he didn't come back, so this poor lad had to work right through until seven at night – six hours at the hardest job on the docks. There were some men from Seaforth in the gang and they took it upon themselves to sort it out, especially one fella who couldn't half dig.

The next morning, the liberty taker was collared at the muster outside the shed and quoted chapter and verse in front of the whole ship. The bosses kept out of it. They knew the score. 'Ye know, you. You're a prick with ears', it began. 'You're a dog's arse. You worked it up an eighteen year old lad. He 'ad te werk from one o'clock 'til seven cos you didn't come back from the Irish club. Well, you're on all day t'day, mate. You're goin' down below now an' you're not comin' up 'til seven o'clock t'night. An' if I see ye face come up out of tha' hatch, I'll fuckin' smack ye off the ladder and you'll go down te the lower hold. D'ye get me?'

The man looked at the floor and shrugged his shoulders. And that's what happened. He worked all day in dreadful conditions. The word was passed around and any liberty takers had second thoughts about doing the same.

Jack Tansey

Tansey was a big man. He had huge hands, and when he shook hands, yours would disappear. He was a gentle giant and well respected down the docks. Tansey had been heavyweight boxing champion in the Royal Navy, and some reckoned that he could well have been a contender for the world title, and this opinion was from men who knew about such things – it was not just wishful thinking. However, the war had destroyed so much promise in a generation.

Tansey was on a bus going towards Bootle from town one Saturday afternoon. He was sitting upstairs on the back seat when he heard two men get on the bus cursing and swearing. They'd obviously had a bit to drink. Tansey had had a few scoops himself but certainly wasn't drunk. The bus moved off and the voices floated up the stairs. A woman objected to the foul language and received a barrage of abuse. Tansey winced when he heard it. This was the late fifties and that sort of language was not tolerated anywhere. Even on the docks where the 'f' word was tolerated and was part of the language, excessive use of expletives was frowned upon.

Another woman mentioned that there were children on the bus who could hear every word, and she in turn received a blast of insults peppered with expletives. The bus drove along Scotland Road towards Lambeth Road, and the men on the lower deck seemed to be enjoying themselves, not caring whom they upset.

Tansey was hoping they would quieten down, but it was a forlorn hope. The bus passed Bankhall and several other women had complained, only to be met by insults of the most obscene kind. The bus conductor wouldn't get involved, as he thought these aggressive 'prigs' might attack him.

Tansey was inwardly fuming and could contain himself no longer. The bus approached the stop at Bedford Road and he could hear them standing on the platform ready to get off when it stopped. He asked the man next to him, 'Would you excuse me, please?' Tansey went down the stairs as the bus stopped and the two men got off. Tansey stepped off behind them. He touched them both on the shoulders simultaneously and when they turned, he threw two punches – Bang, Bang – hitting both of them squarely on the chin. Both men went down as if they had been pole axed and lay prostrate on the pavement by the bus stop.

Tansey stepped back on the bus and rang the bell. The bus groaned away with the people opened mouthed at the speed of it all. The rest of the journey continued quietly as if nothing had happened.

Joe Martini

Martini was reckoned to be the hardest man on the whole line of docks. He had a very deceptive build – one of those men who was tall enough, but at times looked squat because of his body shape. He was broad and carried some weight, and looked like the last man to be able to fight, but fight he certainly could. He had the most devastating punch you could imagine, and stories abounded about his exploits.

In the very late '50s, a professional boxer named Duncan and Martini had an altercation. This led to an arrangement to meet three weeks hence to sort it out at the yard of the Clearing House, which was then on Rimrose Road by its junction with Strand Road. Duncan was as fit as a flea and had a good dig. He was literally fighting fit but still went into training to make sure. Joe Martini, on the other hand, carried on in his usual way, shuffling along to the pub and sinking pints of Guinness, not concerned at all about the impending fight.

The day finally arrived. It was a Thursday, and dockers would rip that ticket from their pay book to go to the Clearing House to pick their wages up. Nobody usually worked overtime on Thursdays. Decades of trying to get men to work after five o'clock when they had money in their pockets had proved fruitless, and over the years it had eventually become normal working practice.

The Clearing House yard was packed, and Duncan had arrived first. He was shadow boxing around to warm up, waiting for Martini to show. He'd been there a few minutes when the buzz went round, 'Martini's here'. Joe walked up, took his overcoat off, and rolled his sleeves up.

A huge circle gathered around to watch the action. Not a word was spoken between the two men and they squared up to each other. Duncan was the first to score with two rapid punches, which caught Martini in the face. Duncan danced back as Martini rocked back on his heels and turned as Duncan circled him, only to rock back again as Duncan with his better boxing ability stepped in and caught Joe twice more.

Eighteen stone and flat-footed people were beginning to wonder if Martini was over the hill. Duncan's supporters were ecstatic. Here was the so-called hardest man on the line of docks being given a boxing lesson and they were howling with derision towards the Martini supporters, who were more or less grouped together watching in grim silence.

Duncan was unconscious before he hit the floor. He'd come bouncing in on his toes and had thrown a right hand towards Joe's chin. It never landed. Martini heaved his right shoulder towards Duncan and at the same time unleashed an unmerciful blow, which caught Duncan right on the point of his jaw. The lights went out immediately and Duncan dropped to the floor. It was obvious that he wouldn't be getting back up and people knelt down on the ground to see to him. It was all over.

Martini, without a flicker of emotion, rolled his shirtsleeves down and buttoned them at the cuffs. He then put his overcoat on, fastened it up, turned, and without a backward glance shuffled away out of the yard. The fight had lasted all of twenty seconds.

Cleared Out

'Down Below. On the deck. On the quay', shouted the ship's boss as the men walked from the muster and filed past the timekeeper to give their numbers in. A group of mainly young dockers were waiting for their hatch number to be called, when one lad told them that his mate, who was in the gang, wouldn't be there as he had the flu. He was asked to tell the hatch boss right away so that a replacement could be sent from the pen.

If they left it too long, any men in the control would have their books stamped AP (Attendance proved) and would be off home until one o'clock, when they would be back looking for work. Meanwhile, their gang would have to work a man short all morning. Besides, anything else it would cock the welt up. You couldn't work with three men on one welt and four men on another. It took two men to handle bags for one thing and numbers had to be even.

'You'd better tell the boss', said an older man. The lad walked over to the hierarchy, who were standing in a small group and told their hatch boss that they were a man short. This particular man was one of those who got a hatch occasionally and was full of his own importance.

He stood with his feet apart with his hands clasped behind his back. An old, black, shortie overcoat was fastened around him, tied with a piece of string and his cap was jammed down on his head. He wore dungarees and his feet were encased in a pair of dull, black Tuff boots planted firmly on the floor. He was living the dream. He'd got a hatch at the Yank.

The lad approached and told him about his friend being ill, and was explaining when he was cut short.

'Get back to ye mates', the man said.

The young man flushed slightly and tried to explain the situation, and was met by, 'Get back to ye mates or you're cleared out'. The lad apologised and tried to explain yet again and was told, 'You're cleared out'. This was a complete abuse of power. This man wanted to make his mark and had chosen this time to do it. The lad went back to his mates and told them what had happened.

'I was only tellin' him we were a man short an' he wouldn't let me finish an' he's cleared me out', he said.

A clearing out was effectively being sacked from that berth, returning to the pen to explain to the control officer and a visit to Ted Bell in box two to face possibly disciplinary action.

The older man who'd told the young docker to inform the hatch boss shouted over, 'Have you just cleared this lad out?' The hatch boss, realising he was on shaky ground gave an almost imperceptible nod of his head.

He was asked the same question again, and this time nodded more noticeably.

'Because if you 'ave', said the older man, 'You'll have te clear us all out. The lad's only tryin' to explain they're a man short. We'll stop the ship'.

At this the hatch boss went white. Here he was; he'd been given a hatch to boss and wanted to rule with an iron hand and show everybody at that hatch who was in charge. He had only been at the ship for one day and he was facing a strike. He was in a no-win situation. If he insisted on sacking the lad he would have a strike on his hands, which would spread in minutes to include all the hatches on the whole ship.

The people responsible with entrusting the hatch to him would be appalled that they could now have a dispute on their hands with the subsequent loss of money and time. If he chose the latter, however, he would face a loss of authority and dignity. He chose the latter. 'Naaaaah. Take no notice', he said. 'He's not cleared out'.

He walked away from the muster of men and hardly appeared for the next four days, keeping himself on the ship out of the way.

Chapter 9
Dirt, Danger, 'n' Disaster

Three Half Crowns

Some jobs down the docks were the most unpleasant of all. One was discharging 'bag' ash. These were heavy sacks of an abrasive ash that had to be carried on men's backs.

The grit would get through their shirts and rub their skin away.

The natural thing to do was to transfer the weight of the bag away from the sore spot in the middle of the back towards a shoulder. This too would get painfully sore, and subsequent bags would be carried on the other shoulder.

At the end of a working day, men would have three spots on their backs with the skin worn off and it was known as 'three half Crowns'. It's not known how they would cope if they had to work on the same commodity the next day. It was excruciating work and was dreaded.

Wet Hides

Cowhides were another nightmare. The hides were sent from abattoirs abroad, and soaked with salt water to keep them from drying out and cracking. The salt water was also to prevent them rotting, as they still had bits of flesh attached to them and the smell was absolutely nauseating. Dockers had to lie down initially on top of the hides and pass a rope snotter around the tails to pull them out with the crane. This was to make a 'sink' in the cargo and make discharging easier.

As the bundles of hides were lifted from the hatch, the stinking water would drip down onto the men like rain and soak them. There were no facilities for them to shower, and there was no protective clothing provided. Men went home in the clothes they'd gone to work in, only this time they were soaked in the stinking salt water and their houses would smell of the hides. It was such a strong smell that one woman swore she could smell her husband coming down the street even before he got to his front door.

Carbon Black

Working with carbon black was also a much-hated job. Inevitably, with hundreds or even thousands of bags coming ashore, there would be some spillage, which would end up on the men's clothes and bodies. It could be washed off, but tended to be absorbed by their skin, and it was said that no matter how much you scrubbed and scrubbed, you could be sitting in a pub that night with a clean white shirt on and it would come out of your pores and you'd have a black tide mark around your collar. Extra money was paid to attempt to compensate the men for these obnoxious cargos, but it was really only a pittance and never did.

Anti Knock

Anti Knock was Ethyl Lead and was a petrol additive. It was exported from Britain, and eventually the empty drums came back to be used again. This was the most dangerous of substances, and it was said that a small amount splashed on you would be absorbed through the skin and would kill you. The empty drums would be lifted out on boards with nets around them. They were painted a light blue colour and had a huge white skull and crossbones painted on them, with a warning in big red letters.

Although empty, they were always treated with respect. It was said that a drum had fallen down below at one foreign port and six men had lost their lives with the contamination. Whether this was true or false, nobody in Liverpool wanted to find out just how poisonous it was.

Anthrax

Other cargos were not so obviously dangerous, but signs in the dock sheds warned of anthrax, which could be contracted through seemingly benign cargos of wool and such, and the notices warned people that if they got a rash between their fingers to report to the medical centre right away.

Snowing Asbestos

The west Alexander Dock was where city boats and sometimes clan boats discharged. One bitterly cold night, a gang of young men had been hired to unload a hatch. The cargo was pigs of copper, so called because when cast, the metal would run down a channel and into the moulds at each side, and it looked for all the world like piglets feeding off a sow. They weren't sure if this cargo of copper qualified for that description, as they were about two feet square and four inches thick and were called 'oven doors'.

The copper cargo was removed and sent ashore in a couple of hours, and the next commodity was ready to be worked at. These were sacks of asbestos that had been compressed with the great weight of copper pressing down. The sacks weren't very big, and were actually quite light. They were, however, hard to remove, but bore the warning: 'Use no hooks'. The dockers found them hard to pull up, and their hands became sore from the rough sacks. Men disregarded the instructions on the sacks and started to use hooks to pick at the ears of the sacks so they could get a grip with their hands. The sacks were of poor quality and tore easily.

After a few slings had been sent up, some of the asbestos could be seen falling back down the hatch like snow. As the unloading progressed, it continued to fall and settled on the men below – on shoulders, heads, and even eyelashes – and put a thin covering on the layers of bags down below. One young lad said, 'I read that this stuff causes cancer. It's bad news'.

Another lad was hooking a sling on to the fall. He called out, 'Heave a bit, driver', and then turned to face the docker who had made the statement. 'D'ye know what. If ye believe everythin' ye read, everythin' causes cancer. I mean ciggies, ale, butter, paint fumes. You name it. Everybody's bloody terrified. Ask yourself this: If this cargo was dangerous, d' ye think for one minute tha' they'd let us be exposed to it with no protection? Ye know, masks and tha'. D'ye think they'd do that?'

The night was bitterly cold, and there was an inch of ice covering the deck, making walking on the ship hazardous. The asbestos was unloaded before seven o'clock and the gang were broke to go home and sleep and be back in the pen the following morning to seek further work. Some felt uneasy about the cargo they'd just handled but pushed it to the back of their minds.

Injuries

Minor (and not so minor) injuries were common. Fingers were always being trapped. One man put his hand up to stop a sling of channel iron swinging, as it could hit a man across the hatch who was talking to someone and didn't have his eye on the ball. At the moment he touched the sling, it tightened up with its own weight and he felt a sting and thought it had pinched him. He instinctively put his hand under his arm and squeezed on it.

The man next to him bent down and said, "Ere y'ar. Here's the top of ye finger', and handed it to him. Compensation would be paid if a firm could be proved to have been negligent. The man took the firm to court and was awarded compensation.

Close Call

There were some unbelievable close calls. A crane driver was eating his lunch and reading the paper on the west side, in one of the large quayside cranes, when a ship being towed into the Gladstone basin hit the quay right by him. With the projection of the bow, it hit the crane and pushed it over. It fell with a huge crash onto the quay and people were amazed to see the driver clambering out unharmed.

The West Side

On the west side, cases of glass were being loaded using the 'married gear'. Loading was going on hour after hour and everybody became just too complacent. The holdsmen were unhooking one end of the wire and letting the deckhands pull it out with the winch. Suddenly, a deckhand gave the winch three notches and turned his eyes away just as the cable snagged under a ringbolt. With the cable now doubled, it was stronger than the ship's fall, and the fall went like a bowstring and snapped.

Men on the quay, and on the next ship, heard that spine tingling scream: 'BELOWWWWW!' They looked and saw the fall wriggling upward, accompanied by a hissing noise. It flew out of the hatch and because it was the 'up and down' cable that had failed, it swung toward the 'yardarm', over the quay, and lashed across the quay with deceptive speed to where three men were having a sly smoke by the shed door. They moved to the right in unison as if choreographed to put themselves just inside the shed door out of harm's way. The cable hit where they'd been standing. A split second later, it curled upwards and hit underneath the top of the open doorway and absolutely blasted a panel out of the roof, which fluttered down at the back of the shed.

There was a moment's silence while men took in what had just happened right out of the blue. The hatch boss where the cable had parted was first to regain his composure. He stood on the deck with both hands on his hips and called across to the three white faces that were now peering around the doorway, 'Go onnnnnn, ye fuckin' cowards', and an absolute explosion of laughter erupted. The men started to gather to look at the damage to the roof and marvel that nobody had been killed or seriously injured.

Exploding Bogey

A gang of young lads who usually worked together were picked to work at the China Berth. Among them were Paddy Kelly, Abraham Lincoln, and Little Boy Blue. At the China Berth, a bogey had been lifted by crane into the loft to move bales of rubber into the next section where they would be stowed. They and the rest of the gang worked all morning, pulling bales off the electric bogey and putting them into designated spaces on the floor. A man would mark them with a brush and purple dye from a large tin ready for putting out when lorries came to collect them.

Lunch hour came and went, and early in the afternoon that part of the cargo had been unloaded from the ship and the men were told to go down to the lower quay to receive a different commodity. Paddy and his mates were told to sling the bogey up and hook it on to the crane so that it could be lifted down to the quay.

A bogey weighed about a ton and was packed under its steel deck with huge batteries. Heavy duty ones could power it all day on innumerable trips up and down the shed and out to the stage end. The method of slinging was to put the ropes between the wheels and the battery box at the front and back. The front one was fixed correctly, but whoever put the back one on put the rope under the driver's step at the end, which was supposed to support a man's weight and nothing more.

'Heave a bit, driver', called one of them, and the crane driver took up the slack in the sling, and then moved the jib out to make sure it was directly over the load. When he was satisfied it wouldn't swing about, he lifted it gently about two feet in the air and raised the crane jib to fetch the bogey clear and lower it to the quay.

He was just about to start lowering it down when a loud creaking noise was heard as the driver's step, no longer able to stand the strain, finally buckled. 'BELOW. BELOOOWWWWWWW', screamed three throats simultaneously as the step bent and the rope slipped off. The back of the Bogey dropped down turned over and fell to the quay thirty feet below, where it literally exploded with the impact and burst into dozens of pieces.

A Chinese crewman was walking up the quay and hadn't noticed the crane lifting anything from the loft.

He was practically underneath when he heard the warning shouts. He saw the bogey above him falling out of the sling and literally ran for his life. The Chinese weren't noted for producing Olympic sprinters, but this one was the exception!

As it was, nobody was injured and everybody came to look at the wreck. The three young dockers were reported and had to go and see Ted Bell in box two, who saw to discipline. No action was taken when it was realised that they'd had no training at all in procedures, as it had been assumed that they knew how to sling things. It wasn't until a year later that all employees starting work on the docks had to go to school for a week to learn safe working practices.

Tragedy

Amidst all the hustle and bustle of the Liverpool docks, tragedy was never far away. Cargo was lifted over men's heads and powerful machinery was always in close proximity. Rubber bales became misshapen with the pressure from cargo above and ropes would literally fly off when a 'putter out, was lowering them onto a lorry on the side of the shed away from the ship.

A young man had been killed outright on his first morning down the docks. He was twenty-four years old and a bale of rubber fell from the loft and struck him on the head and shoulders. His father worked down at the docks and had pushed to get his son a 'book'. People said he was never the same man again. He blamed himself for getting his son the job.

At the China Berth, an elderly man was pulling bales of rubber up slightly so that the men could get their trucks underneath. The French chalk used to stop the bales from sticking together in the hold got everywhere, and with the crane swinging the nets in through the door of the loft, it was over an inch thick in the doorway.

Rain had been falling all morning, and the wind blew it into the loft through the door. The chalk became like white mud and made it slippery underfoot. The man edging the bales up was working facing into the loft instead of toward the open door. He pulled at the top of a bale of rubber for the next trucker in line to push the blade of the truck underneath and the hook slipped as he pulled. He slipped in the mud as he stumbled back, and fell over the edge of the loft and down onto the quay thirty feet below.

A man working on the deck of the ship literally jumped from the ship's rail down to the quay to help him and took his false teeth out so he could breathe better. The ambulance was there in no time and took the poor man away.

Big Paddy Connor (O'Connor) was the quay foreman at W H Bowes. Paddy rushed up to St Joan's church for the priest then went straight to the hospital. Sadly, the man died minutes later, and the news came back to the gang. It had been his birthday that very day. He was sixty-one. Some of the younger men were upset that the ship continued working even though a man had been killed. The hatch boss was embarrassed. He'd had no instructions to the contrary.

'What can you do? What can you do?' was all he could say, and he stood there wringing his hands in response to suggestions that the whole ship should stop for the day as a mark of respect. It wasn't a case of men using it as an excuse to get off work. It was a genuine wish to show some common decency when a man they'd been working with had just lost his life.

The ship continued discharging as if nothing had happened. Younger dockers looked to the older men for guidance, but it wasn't forthcoming, and not knowing what to do, they worked until knocking off time at seven o'clock that night. The next day a replacement was sent from the pen to make the gang up to the right number.

There were men employed by the 'National Dock Labour Board' who should never have been classed fit for work and certainly not down the Liverpool docks. One man was literally deaf and dumb. He was killed when a huge sheet of steel swept across the deck and took him and the ship's rail into the water. A diver had to go down to sling the steel up and lift it. They recovered the man's body from underneath it at the same time. He hadn't heard the shouted warning that might have afforded him time to move out of the way.

Falling down below was not uncommon. Ships were huge and the drop to the lower hold was great. Working down below was dangerous, and holdsmen were injured more than any other dockers.

Two men were working down below at a Colony boat, loading cases of glass for Australia. The cases were all different sizes and because they were loading the 'deep port' cargo (first in, last out), the cargo had to come up level. It was an absolute work of art and very skilled. Motor cars might be going on top of it all, and ships roll at sea. If the cargo shifted, it could lead to catastrophe. When this sort of stowing was completed, the expression used to be "Eh, lads. Come and inspect the ballroom', and it would be completely level right across the ship.

The two men were picking the cases out to make it all correct, and they had a case of glass that they thought might fit into a space perfectly. One man shouted up to the man, passing the word, 'Heave a bit. A small inch'. The man on deck gave the hand signal to heave the slightest bit, and the two men down below were discussing whether the case would fit or jam.

One man said, 'D'ye think it'll go, Billy?' Billy took a step back to get a better idea, and that step saved his life. In an instant, a huge shadow passed between them, inches from his face. A hatch board the size of a living room floor and bound with brass had fallen from the top of the hatch into the lower hold. His friend took the full force of it on his shoulders and the back of his head and was killed instantly. Screams followed to send a box down, and he was taken up out of the hatch and put into the ambulance, which arrived within minutes.

Billy went in the ambulance with him and he was sitting in the hospital when a nursing sister came out to talk to him. She said, 'You know your friend is dead, don't you?'

Billy told her, 'I knew it the minute he was struck. If I hadn't stepped back at that instant, it would have been me as well'. She pushed a large whisky into his hand and told him to drink it.

What had happened left the firm wide open. The beams across the hatch fitted into slots welded to the sides at the top. Holes in the brackets coincide with a hole in the beam and a steel pin goes through the lot to make sure the beam can't lift out if it's touched by cargo coming out of the hold.

At some time in the ship's history, a pin had been bent and as a result had become difficult to insert, so it had been left out. Only half the hatch was uncovered, and as the driver heaved a little, the huge 'ball' on the steel cable (more of a cigar shape and fitted to keep the steel hawser free of 'roses') caught the side of the beam and lifted it out of the bracket. The beam moved over, allowing the huge hatch board to fall between it and the next beam along and down onto the two holdsmen.

Lie after lie was told by all and sundry to protect the firm. Billy fought the case for the man's widow even when the union backed off, deeming the case unwinnable, and he proved that the crew, the mate, the captain, and the firm knew that there was no pin in the beam. He won the case and she was awarded a pension. The woman thanked him profusely and offered him money when it was all over. He declined the offer and told her, 'You'll be needin' that ye self, Queen'.

He said later, 'I had someone's prayers with me that day when the hatch board passed in front of me face. God be good to him'.

The Parthia

The dry dock, or as it was more commonly known, 'the Graving Dock' was a little to the right of the Gladstone gate. There were posts around it with chains slung in between, along its whole length except for the far end, where the ships came into it from the Gladstone basin.

Ships needing repair or inspection would be towed in and the gates would be closed. The water would be pumped out and the ship would be lowered onto the line of blocks that extended for nearly all of its length. Other blocks would be pulled in from the sides with winches and chains to choc the ship and make it stable. The water would then be pumped out and the ship would settle.

The Graving dock could take the biggest of ships, but 'Not the Queens', it was said. 'The Queen Elizabeth' and 'Queen Mary' operated out of Southampton where the water was deeper.

The Gladstone could not take ships of 80,000 tons with a length of nearly a quarter of a mile. Liverpool could take the biggest ships afloat at the 'landing stage' at the pier head but not inside the docks themselves. The 'Empress Boats' of Canadian Pacific Railways (CPR) would discharge passengers at the floating landing stage, and then move down and through the Gladstone lock into their own berth in order to discharge the small amount of cargo and mail.

These were beautiful ships with gleaming white paintwork and yellowish buff-coloured funnels. They sailed regularly across the Atlantic and into the great lakes of Canada. There was never much work for the dockers at these vessels.

Their primary purpose was to carry passengers, not cargo, and two days at the CPR was about all that could be hoped for. Dockers would then be 'broke' and sent back to the pool of labour in the pen to seek further work.

The Parthia was not a big ship, but big enough. Nor was she a beautiful ship. She wasn't a graceful queen of the sea. She was a working cargo boat, and was sitting in the dry dock with her complete shape visible. There was an industrial dispute between the ship repairing gangs and their employers. The men had waited until the Parthia was settled in the Graving Dock and taken one of the propellers off to facilitate repairs. They then went on strike. The employers couldn't send the ship to another repair facility or even move her out of the dock. The dock was now blocked to other ships and the men had the whip hand.

The Parthia sat there for weeks while negotiations continued and the pools of water on the concrete floor of the facility that were always visible had dried up. The mass of equipment surrounding her now stood idle and rusting, and the dock was filled with an eerie silence.

Access to the Graving Dock was by concrete steps that had openings on the quay. Flights of steps were connected by small landings, and each landing had what looked like a doorway facing into the dock, with a steel bar across for safety.

The dock was about eighty feet from the quay to the bottom and the two staircases on each side of the dock allowed normal access to the keel of the ship. Work would sometimes be carried out on the deck or inside the vessel at the same time, and a gangway would be placed from the quay across to the ship. Crossing the gangway with no water underneath made people realise how far down it was.

It was decided to move the gangway, and two ship repairers had slung it up for the crane to lift. When they hooked it on and the crane had heaved slightly to take the weight and make sure it was safe, the ropes securing it to the ship were removed and the crane started to lift it.

The men who'd slung it had stayed on the gangway because they would have to hook it off from the crane when it had been moved along. Imagining it would stay straight and level, they were in the middle of the companionway when it suddenly bucked up at one end. They were caught by surprise and one man didn't have hold of the rail and grabbed at his mate as he fell towards the low end. The other man had tight hold of the rail but his hands were pulled away by the other man's weight and both of them fell down to the concrete floor of the dry dock.

The first man to fall, it was said, landed half on his side and survived, although he was badly injured. The other man had no such luck. He landed on his feet and was killed outright, and him with a young wife just a few weeks pregnant, and with a little boy and girl on the floor too. A sombre mood enveloped the docks for weeks after, and men were a bit subdued. His wife was a small, slim, quiet girl, and she retreated into herself, her pregnancy becoming more and more visible as the weeks and months passed. It was an ever-present reminder of an awful tragedy.

Chapter 10
Dockers Had Some Stories

There's a Place for Us

The following story was recounted in the crew's quarters of a coaster at the Yankee Berth, where the dockers had taken refuge from the rain during the night. The order had been shouted to 'Cover up', and one young, day-old chick had remarked that the employers were very considerate to let the men get out of the rain. There were a few chuckles from the men huddled in the warm cabin at the young man's naivety, and a holdsman squashed in the corner with two hands round a mug of tea spoke up.

'They don't give a shit about you, son', he said. 'We're loadin' coils of steel wire, and it'll go rusty if it gets wet. That's why we've covered the hatch up. No other reason. If we were loadin' timber, you'd be out there now, soaked to the skin, as would all of us'.

Most of the men grunted in agreement, as there was never any love lost between the management and the workforce. There was a short silence as he mulled over what had just been said. A deckhand called Ernie broke the silence.

"Ey, I meant to tell ye', he began in a scouse accent you could cut with a knife. 'Did ye 'ear about Stan last week? Ye wouldn't believe it'.

The background to this was that Ernie could play a guitar and he worked with Stan doing the clubs at the weekend. Stan also worked on the docks. He certainly wasn't the best of club acts, but he was reliable and filled a slot on the bill. He wasn't the tallest of men and he carried a bit of weight.

Ernie continued: 'We were workin' on that big club in Walton Sat'day night, an' we had the club's drummer and organist with us, an' I was playin' me Hofner blonde like, Lecky, ye know'.

Ernie always threw a mention of his guitar into any conversation about music or the clubs. He knew that people would be impressed by the fact that he had so much faith in his playing that he would be confident enough to buy such a prestigious instrument.

'We started off with a few songs an' tha", he continued, 'then Stan did his bit of patter an' we were doin' all right. Most people seemed to be enjoyin' it except for one owl girl sittin' right in front of us. Jeez. Whatever joke Stan told she would shout out, "I've heard it", dead loud so everyone in the place could 'ear 'er, an' she's only sittin' right by us.

'Anyway, Stan tells another one and the same shout comes from this owl cow: "I've heard it". Stan did another one and the same thing happened. Now ye know Stan's easy goin', but I know him an' I can see he's gettin' rattled even though he's got tha' big plastic smile on his face. Anyway he says, 'Okay, okay. Here's one you haven't heard', an' he told this joke and all the people laughed except this woman in the front, who shouted, "I fell out me cot laughin' at that one". Stan suddenly lost it and shouted down to 'er, "Well ye must 'ave landed on ye face, ye ugly owl bastard".

'All the people were laughin', but I told Stan to back off, as this one might 'ave a couple of sons with her, or maybe her husband is a handy lad still and we could end up fightin' our way out of the place. An' I've got me Hofner blonde guitar with me. Lecky, ye know'. He imitated the strumming of a guitar.

'Anyway, we did a couple more songs and came to Stan's impression spot. Stan said te me out of the corner of his mouth, "This'll slay 'em". He didn't think for a minute he could be so close te the truth. Stan has to tell the audience who it is he's trying to impersonate or they might never guess. He starts off with James Stewart. Ye know, all that "Aaaaah, Aaaaah, Aaaaah stuff".

'Then he shouts out "Ray Charles", an' he's got the black tights over his head with the sunglasses on, and he's stumblin' round the stage. That went down well, an' he did a few others. When he shouted out "James Mason", someone shouted out, "Who's he?"

'Anyway, we came te the high spot of the act where Stan really knocks them dead. "Ladeeeeeze an' chunnellllmennnn, Mr P.J. Proby", an' Stan walks out. An' I must admit, he looked the part. He 'ad a wig on with a big bow in the back and was wearin' a pair of black tights, an' around his wrists he 'ad two pieces of lace curtain held on by elastic bands. He had one of those ruff things ye can buy fastened te the front of his white shirt, an' he walked up to the mike.

'Now I don't know if any of ye know that club, but whoever lays it out must 'ave been in the army, cos all the tables are laid out in dead straight lines. They must do it with a piece of string because from the stage ye can see how neat it all is tables goin' away in the darkness with an inch between each one, and the other rows across the club exactly the same'.

The men in the cabin were taking all this in and visualising the scene.

Ernie explained further: 'At the front of the stage they've got these footlights. Not real ones, but one of the members made this curved metal frame up in their place in Kirkby one Sat'day mornin' on the sly. It went from one side of the stage te the other, and it had 100 watt bulbs in it. On the top, they put wrought iron te make it look posh.

'Anyway, it's last orders at the bar, an' everyone's doublin' up, and the tables are groanin' with ale. There's ale for dogs an' the place is packed out. Stan started te sing tha' song from 'West Side Story', is it! 'Somewhere'. The place goes quiet, an' 'e kicks off. "There's a plaaaaace for uuusssssss ... sommmmmawheeeeeeere. A plaaaaace for uuusssssss", just like P.J. Proby. I mean it's his best one. 'E always saves it 'til near the end.

'Anyway, Stan decides te jump over the footlights and go down on one knee te the owl one who was hecklin' him and sing te her. What he didn't see was the wrought iron on top of the footlights, cos it didn't catch the lights, cos they'd painted it black. He must 'ave caught his toe in the top and all I saw was Stan's arse disappearin' inte the darkness.

He didn't land on his feet an' stumble. No, nothin' like that. He came down like a friggin' bomb. Like an Olympic diver with his feet together an' up in the air, an' his arms stretched out in front of him with his palms facin' forward, ready for the impact.

'Anyway, Stan's fifteen stone, and he hit the edge of the first table with a thump. It was like an explosion. There was, like, this spray of ale that went out, an' everyone got a bit. Because the tables 'ad this little gap between them, they hit each other like a sort of chain reaction and it sounded, "Ratatatatatatatatatatatat", right down to the end of the row of tables, an' most of the people fell over backwards off their chairs and fell on the floor.

'Well! They must 'ave all been drinkin' Guinness, cos there must 'ave been forty pints of it that went over all at once.

'There was this big pool of Guinness that looked like black engine oil in a circle that was spreadin' over the floor with a white ring 'round it from the froth, an' all these people lyin' in it. The owl bastard who'd been givin' us a hard time was on her back, tryin' te ge' up. She was saturated in ale.

'The place exploded inte laughter like you've never heard before, and people sittin' at the lines of tables who weren't affected were standin' on the chairs for a better look. Everybody was convulsin' with laughter. The organist and drummer 'ad tried to keep playin' like true pros, but after a little while they had te stop an' were screwed up with laughter.

'Fuckin' 'ell. Ye know what happened then? Out of the middle of all this carnage, all the smashed glass and people lyin' in the beer, Stan emerged with the wig on sideways and the bow was over his left ear. His white shirt was soaked in Guinness and was dark brown. An' I couldn't believe it. He still 'ad hold of the mike and he carried on as if nothin' 'ad happened.

'"Peace and quiet an' open air. Wait for uuuss sssss sommmmmawheeeeeeere".

'This kicked off another scream of laughter from the audience, an' people were laughin' for a good ten minutes, and then it would die down, An' then swell up again.

'Anyway, Stan hurt his side so we went te Walton Hospital and they X-rayed him an' found out he'd broken a rib. An' the worst part was that when I went for the money the next day, they told me to beat it because of the damage'.

SAS

Bobby was in his mid thirties. He was a porter on the docks and worked mainly on the quay. He'd had a hard time a while before, and those close to him kept quiet about it to save him any embarrassment. Bobby lived with his mother and sister near the docks, and had a small circle of friends. He'd never had a girlfriend that anyone knew about until he met a woman and fell for her in a big way. Against the advice from his family, he was married six weeks later.

Bobby and his new bride took off for a honeymoon in Germany. They met some British holidaymakers over there, and after a few days his wife went off with one of the men in the party, taking all of Bobby's money and even his passport.

He was devastated and didn't know what to do. He was ashamed to go home, and was absolutely humiliated to think that he was stranded in Germany and penniless.

He'd gone over to Germany in his car and didn't have enough petrol to go far. In desperation, he went to an army camp he'd noticed nearby and went to the guardhouse to ask for help.

He was soon taken before the adjutant, who told him not to worry, and that they would fix him up with accommodation for that night and would contact the British consul the next morning to sort things out. He was given an army bed in a small billet in which he was the only occupant.

The next day, the adjutant saw him and told him that it would be a couple of days to sort the paperwork out, and if he wanted, he could work in the kitchens, as they had civilian workers on the camp and he could earn some money in the meantime. Bobby readily agreed and thanked the man. He was taken down to the cookhouse and introduced to the chef, who was also a corporal. He was shown what to do and after a short while found that they got on well together.

Bobby worked in the kitchen for a few days, and Friday night the chef said he would take him out for a drink. There was a corporal's mess in the camp, and as a guest he was taken in and introduced to some of the other serving soldiers. They were kindness itself, and plied Bobby with drinks while he recounted the story. One of the other corporals was from Birkenhead, so Bobby didn't feel that he was so much out on a limb. He was trying to buy a round of drinks but they kept telling him to put his money away. Presently the corporal, walked away from the bar to talk to someone he knew for a minute and Bobby was left on his own. He'd sunk a few pints of beer by this time and was swaying with one hand grasping the edge of the counter.

He asked the steward behind the bar for another pint of beer, and was refused. The steward told him that he wasn't allowed to buy drinks there and really shouldn't be in the place. Bobby asked again, and again was refused service.

With the alcohol and what had happened over the recent past, he reacted. The IRA had mounted operations against British soldiers and military installations across Europe, and Bobby, even in his inebriated state, had this fact in his mind.

'Listen here, you little shit', he said. 'I'm from twenty-two squadron Special Air Service. I've been sent here to protect you because you can't do it yourselves, now give us a pint'.

The steward paled and complied. Bobby paid him and poured the beer down in one. People in the bar had heard what he'd said and the whole place went quiet. He realised that it might be a good idea to leave, and he walked over to the nearest door and turned the handle, hoping that it wasn't a broom cupboard. He was relieved that the door opened on to a long room with a wood parquet floor with tables arranged around the walls.

It was a warm summer's night, and the sash windows were wide open, with lace curtains moving gently with the evening breeze. Looking about, he saw that there was no other way out except through the door he'd entered by. He decided to exit through a window, walk across the grass, and make his way back to the billet and his bed. A party of soldiers, curious as to what he was up to, opened the door and peered in, just as Bobby jumped out of the window. The problem was, he'd forgotten that when he'd entered the mess earlier, he'd had to walk up two flights of stairs to get to the bar and the window was thirty feet up in the air and not on the ground floor. He went down and landed mostly on his back with a loud thud.

He couldn't get his breath and was opening and closing his mouth like a goldfish. He stretched his arm across his body and clutched at the ivy that covered that side of the building. He managed to roll under the overhanging foliage out of view of anyone above.

The soldiers who looked and had seen him jump out couldn't believe what they'd just witnessed. They ran to the window and peered out. Not being able to see him, they assumed he'd melted into the darkness. Bobby was as silent as possible, still fighting for breath, and heard one of them say, 'It's the special air service, isn't it. They know how to fall'.

Eddie Flanagan

Eddie was an ex-seafarer, and probably one of the greatest comedians to come out of Liverpool. One docker who said he was a mate of Eddies recounted some of his jokes and stories.

Speaking Spanish

On one trip, Eddie's ship arrived in a South American port to find the port workers on strike. There was one solitary figure on the quay, wrapped in a blanket, and looking as if he was sleeping. The ship had to be berthed and the skipper asked if anybody among the crew could speak Spanish. One young Liverpool deckhand said that he could (although he couldn't). The captain asked the lad to shout across to this man to put the rope over the bollard when it was thrown.

'Okay', the lad said. ''Ey, Lario. Put the ropio over the bollardio when we throwio'.

Gales of laughter came from the crew on deck. The figure on the quay stirred and called something back.

'What did he say?' the captain asked the lad.

'He can't. He's still on his dinner hour', he replied.

Trust You

Eddie took his wife up to Scotland for a week in a caravan. 'It did nothin' but rain all day Monday, and me bride sat starin' out of the window. All day. Same thing Tuesday, Wednesday, Thursday. Just staring. Not a word. Friday mornin' it was still rainin', an' she spoke for the first time in days.

She said, "Trust you". Later on, she said tha' we'd been there since Monday and she could do with a change of scenery. I put a coat over me head and went outside and dragged the caravan 'round to face the other way'.

Me Judie

'I was in the wine lodge with me Judie. She asked me if I loved her, an' I told her of course I did. She said she'd seen a lovely, thick gold bracelet in the jeweller's window, and could I get it for her.

I went out and got a brick off the debris and put it through the window and came back into the wine lodge and gave it to her. She was delighted, and said she'd seen a mink coat in a shop in Bold Street and she would love that as well. I got another brick off the debris and smashed the window and brought the coat back and gave it to her.

There she was, sitting wearin' this fabulous mink coat and gold bracelet in the wine lodge, lookin' like a million dollars. She said she'd also noticed a lovely, expensive gold and diamond ladies' wrist watch in another jeweller's window, and could she 'ave tha' as well. I 'ad te tell her, 'Ar, 'ey, queen. D'ye think I'm made of bricks?'

No Pain

There were two mates sinking down loads of Aussie whites in Moorfields and feeling no pain. One fella said that he could fly, and that it was just mind over matter and he would prove it.

They staggered outside, followed by a few interested drinkers, and he climbed up on the wall, flapped his arms, and dived off head first onto the pavement. He was taken to hospital with a gash on his head and a tooth missing. The next day, the friend he'd been with went to visit him in hospital and was asked, 'Ye knew I was drunk. Why didn't ye stop me?'

His mate said, 'Stop ye? I had a tenner on ye'.

Doctor Wit

There was a consultant in a Liverpool hospital. He really was a top cat, and had a certain way with him that demanded respect. He was a gastrologist, and all the people with stomach troubles would to go to him.

A docker from box two had an appointment to see him, and he would be first in so he asked the lads on the docks to keep the job going and he would only be away an hour at the most the next morning. He was in the waiting room first, and the doctor was a couple of minutes late so the room had filled up with patients. The doctor swept in and went to the receptionist, who handed him a list of appointments. He looked up and down the list, and then turned to this docker and said, 'Are you waiting to see me?' The guy jumped to his feet, respectfully pulling his cap off his head as he did so. 'Yes', he replied. The doctor asked him right out of the blue, 'When did you last have sex?'

'Ermmmmm, Ermmmmmmm. Last Friday', he spluttered with his face like a beetroot. The doctor walked into his office and closed the door, leaving the fella standing in the middle of a packed and silent waiting room, with twenty people staring at him with interest.

Chapter 11
Wokky's Tall Stories

When it rained down the docks and ships were loading or unloading cargos that might be damaged, the order was given to 'Cover up'. Hatch boards were replaced, and if the rain was severe, canvas sheets would be pulled over them in turn.

If men were working at night, there was nowhere for them to go, and they usually sought refuge in the crew's quarters or the engine room, where it was warm and dry. Milk, sugar, and tea would be pooled and mixed together in any large tin that could be found, and the engineers would oblige by filling it up with clean boiling water. Tea never tasted so good. Men would get themselves comfortable as they sipped their tea, and some rolled cigarettes as they basked in the comfort of doing nothing and getting paid for it.

It was at times like this that the stories would start to come out–about war experiences, in the army or the merchant navy, with the gentle whine of the ship's generators providing power for the lights and winches as a backdrop.

'Wokky' told the most incredible tall stories, and men would hang on every word. A silence, if it could be called that, would descend on the assembled company and he would begin.

Wokky in Manhattan

'Our Vera was a G.I. bride, and me and me tart were over there visitin' her and her fella. I was walkin' 'round that Manhattan, and as I was goin' past the back door of that Waldorf Astoria, the door opened and the chef came out, leaned against the wall, and broke his heart cryin'. I went up to him and put me arm on his shoulder and said, "There, don't be upshettin' ye self. Things can't be tha' bad".

'He turned when he heard me voice and said, "Wokky, thank God I've seen ye. I don't know what I'm gonna do. In there tonight I've got John Kennedy, Frank Sinatra, Dean Martin, and Sammy Davis Junior, and all their wives, and they've told me that they've eaten the finest and most exotic foods in the world you care to mention, and seeing as this is the world famous Waldorf

Astoria, they want me to prepare something really fabulous that they've never had before. Wokky, I've racked my brains and I can't come up with any ideas. Wokky, what am I going to do?"

"'Stop cryin', for a start", I said. "Go back in and give the head waiter some money and tell him te go down the market and get a cabbage and a sheet of ribs".

'When the waiter came back, I went in the kitchen and showed him how te make spare ribs and cabbage, and it was taken out and served. I saw the chef when he came back in later, and he said, "Wokky, how can I ever thank you enough? They all cleared their plates and told me it was the best food they'd ever tasted, and when I was walking back into the kitchen, I saw John Kennedy and Frank Sinatra licking their fingers"'.

Wokky the Navigator

'Me and Alice had a week in Benidorm, and we were flyin' home into Speke Airport. The plane got over Liverpool and was circlin' about for ages when the stewardess came up and said, "Wokky, we're over Liverpool but the pilot can't find the airport. He asked me to ask you if you'll go on the flight deck and help him find it".

"'shertainly", I said. So I went down te the front of the plane and got on the flight deck. The pilot saw me and said, "Wokky, thank God you're on board. I can't seem to find the airport and we're running low on fuel. You know Liverpool. Can you direct me, please?"

"'No problem", I said. "Now let's see where we are". So I looked out the window and said, "Right. If ye look down there, that's the Rice lane flyover by Walton church. Your goin' the wrong way, so turn around".

'He did, and I said, "That's more like it. Now here we are, goin' over the Flyover again. Now there's a set of traffic lights at Walton Hall Avenue and ye continue over them and get onto Queen's Drive and keep goin' through all the lights until ye get to the flyover by Broadgreen hospital by the end of the M62.

"'Keep goin', keep goin', until ye get to the roundabout by Childwall Fiveways and take the second turn left off the roundabout, and keep goin' until ye get te the traffic island. Turn left onto Allerton Road, and follow the road all the way down past Paul McCartney's old house te the lights just after the railway bridge. Turn left there, and then right at the lights, and ye come te the beginnin' of the main runway at Speke airport. And there ye are: home and dry".

'The plane landed and all the passengers started clappin' and cheerin' with relief. The pilot was so grateful he said, "Wokky, thank you so much. Is there anything I can do for you?" so I said, "If it's not too much trouble, can ye phone me a taxi?"'

Wokky at the Grand National

Dockers were mostly not what we now call racist. Ships came into Liverpool from all over the world with crews of different backgrounds, languages, and colours, and all were mostly respected. Wokky would never refer to anyone as being black or coloured. He had his own expression, and that was 'stowaway'.

'I was havin' a bevy with me bride in the Chaser by Fazakerley hospital', he said, 'and I noticed two little stowaways sittin' in the far corner nursin' a half pint each. I felt sorry for them and asked the barmaid te find out what they'd like te drink. She came back and said they'd like a couple of brown mixed, so I had it sent over.

'Later on, when they were goin', one of them stopped by our table and put two tickets down, and he thanked me for bein' so kind and said would I please use the tickets and he would see me tomorrow. I didn't have me readin' glasses with me, so I glanced at the tickets and put them in me pocket.

'The next day, I remembered the tickets and had a look what they were for. They were for the Grand National at Aintree that day, and were for the main stand.

'Anyway, me and Alice gets up there in the afternoon, goes te the main stand, and hands the tickets in. The man on the door says that it's not for here, "Sir". It's for the VIP lounge, and we're shown to another door with flunkies clearing people out of our way, and shown upstairs to a beautiful lounge with a large dinin' table with candlesticks on it, ready for a fabulous meal to be served. Two men walked up with their wives and greeted us, and I recognised them as the two stowaways from the Chaser the day before. They introduced themselves.

'"Wokky, so glad you came!" they said. "It was nice of you to buy us a couple of brown mixed yesterday. I'm the Agar Khan, and this is my brother, the Ali khan (two of the richest men in the world), and this is my wife, Rita Heyworth (heiress to the Woolworth billions). Sit down and enjoy a beautiful meal while you watch the national. Anything you'd like to drink is here, from the finest champagne to the most expensive Napoleon brandy. You are our revered guests".

'So, we sat down and enjoyed a wonderful afternoon. Later on, the Agar Khan leaned over and asked me would I allow him a great favour, as a little band started up in the corner. I told him yes, anythin' he wished. He asked me if he could have a dance with Alice. "Certainly", I told him, and asked him, "Can I have a dance with Rita?"'

Wokky the Electrician

'I was workin' at a colony boat, and one of the ship's winches had packed in. Two fellas from Campbell and Isherwood's had been tryin' te fix it all mornin' and were havin' no joy. They'd phoned up and two of the bosses had come down te have a look, and they couldn't figure it out either.

They were standin' there, scratchin' their heads, when I was goin' past on me bike. One of them saw me and shouted, "Wokky, thank God we seen ye. Can you come and have a look at this for us?" I went aboard and they had this winch stripped down. The main man said, "Wokky, this has got us beat. There's power going in. We've checked all that and all the connections are good, but it just won't turn".

'I said, "Let's have a little look", and I found the fault right away. I told them to think of what they'd been taught as young apprentices, and I

171

went through it with them. I reminded them that there were magnets fastened to the inside of the casin', and as the armature revolved between them, a current was induced. A wire was fed back to the magnets, and this in turn stepped up the magnetism, which induced a stronger current in the armature, and so on. They all agreed that that is how it worked, but asked me what the problem was. And I told them, "Gentlemen. The problem is that there is no residual magnetism in the magnets, and the molecules will have to be exited in one of the magnets to make it work", which I duly did. They put the winch back together, switched on the power, and it worked like a dream'.

There was a silence from his enthralled audience, until someone rose to the bait and asked, 'Wokky, how did you excite the molecules in the magnet?' Wokky drank the last drop of tea from his cup and said, 'I hit it with me 'ammer'.

Wokky in Hollywood

'I was in New York with me bride te see our Vera an her fella, and they took us on holiday in America te Hollywood where all the film stars live. We were walkin' along one day and we saw a crowd of people gathered around what seemed like someone makin' a film, so we went over te take a look.

We were at the back of the crowd, and I stood on tiptoe te see what was goin' on, and in the middle was John Wayne with Maureen O'Hara, surrounded by cameras and lights. John Wayne caught sight of me over the heads and shouted, "Wokky, Wokky, thank God I seen you", and then, "Let Wokky through".

'I got through and John said, "Wokky, what a day I'm having. The script says that I've got to kiss Maureen, but the director is saying that I'm not doing it right. Wokky, can you please show me how it's done?"

"'Certainly, John", I said. "Just stand aside and watch closely".

'The director said he would run the cameras te capture it on film so that John could watch it later, and called out, "Lights. Camera. Action".

'I held Maureen in me arms, leaned her back, and planted a big kiss on her lips, and then lifted her up again. Maureen's eyes had flickered when I kissed her, and she said, "Oh, Wokky. Oh, Wokky, that was wonderful".

'She asked the director if he'd make her a copy te keep for herself. The crowd and all the camera crew broke out into a big round of applause, and John Wayne turned around and said, "Wokky,

173

if you hadn't turned up here today I don't know what I'd have done. It might have taken us a week to get it right. Is there anything I can do for you?"

'I said, "Actually, John, I could murder a pint"'.

Wokky Meets Tarzan

Johnny Weissmuller was the first screen Tarzan, and also a great swimmer.

'I was in America', Wokky said, 'stayin' in this big, posh hotel, and they had this great big swimmin' pool there. Open air, and there were all kinds of Judies around. Real lookers. After a bit, I thought I'd have a swim and I dived in the pool. I did a few lengths usin' the eight beat Australian crawl, and after a bit noticed everybody lookin' at me. This fella was surrounded by Judies, and he walked over te the edge of the pool and spoke te me as I got out. He said, "Wokky, I'm Johnny Weissmuller. You might have seen me on the pictures. I'm Tarzan in the films". We shook hands and I said, "What can I do for ye, John?"

'He said, "Wokky, I'm supposed to be a bit of an owl swimmer, but I can't swim as good as you. How do you swim so fast?"

'I said te him, "It's not a big secret, John. It's somethin' the Aussies do called the eight beat crawl".

'He said, "Wokky, can you do me a favour? Can you learn me to do the eight beat Australian crawl?"

'I said, "No, John. I'll teach ye. You'll have to learn yourself".

'A while after, when we got back home, I went te see the latest Tarzan film, and sure enough he was fightin' a shark in this big lagoon, and I noticed he was doin' the eight beat Australian crawl chasin' after it, and I thought, "I taught him that"'.

Wokky and the Indian Chief

'Anyway, like I was tellin' ye, the day after I taught Johnny Weissmuller the eight beat Australian crawl, I was walkin' 'round, lookin' for presents te take home, and I went in this bar for a swift half and got a bevy. I saw this red Indian sittin' in the corner. Ye know, all the feathers and buckskins an' all tha'. I said te the barman, "Who's he?'

'The barman said, "Hiya, Wokky. He's the memory man. He can answer any question on sport you can think of. Anything at all".

'So I thought, "Well, I'll catch him out. He won't know anythin' about football in England".

So I goes over and I says te him, "Can ye tell me who won the FA cup in England in 1965?"

'Without hesitation, he says, "Liverpool".

'Well, I was very impressed. I mean, how would a Red Indian know that? So I says te him, "Who did they beat?"

'He says, "Leeds United at Wembley".

'"Well", I thought. "What was the score?" I asked.

'He said, "Two one to Liverpool in extra time. Ian St John scored the winner".

'I was amazed at this man's memory. Anyway, te cut a long story short, I was back in America two years later and I found the same bar, and true enough, the same red Indian was sittin' in the same corner. I went over and thought I would greet him in the Indian manner. I put the palm of me hand up and said, "How".

'He said, "It was a diving header into the near corner".

Wokky and the Queen

Wokky was holding court again. The deckhands were moving derricks about, leaving the holdsmen some time to sit and talk down below.

'I was in Balliol Road in Bootle last week, and the pavements were crowded with people, and all the kids with little union jacks, an' police cars everywhere. I asked this woman what was goin' on, and she said, "Hiya, Wokky. The Queen's coming te Bootle today. It's been in the Bootle Times".

'So I thought te me self, "Well, I might as well wait and see what goes on".

'Anyway, within a few minutes, a procession of big posh cars arrives with all them bobbies on motorbikes alongside, and they glide to a stop right by where I'm standin'. D'ye know what 'ad happened? The Queen's Rolls Royce 'ad got a puncture.

'It turned out that the spare wheel in the boot was flat, and they'd got no jack as well, so they couldn't move. The chauffeur 'ad told the Queen what 'ad happened, and she was just sittin' there, not knowin' what te do. The police didn't have a clue either. The Queen looked over an' spotted me. She wound the window down and shouted out, "Wokky, thank God I seen you".

'I said, "Oright, Queen".

'She said, "Wokky, we've got a flat tyre and the spare wheel's flat. I'm on my way to Seaforth to unveil a plaque in a sheltered accommodation place, and I can't turn up in a police car. All the old people will be upset if I don't turn up in the Rolls. Wokky, can you please help me?"

"Shertainly", I shaid. "I know it's Sat'day an' most places are closed, but send the bobbies down te the back of Crosby Town hall. There's a fella there that does weddin's an' funerals. Say I sent them and could he lend us the spare wheel off his Rolls Royce. And on the way back, call into Ted's timber and pick up a piece of timber as long as ye can get. About two inches thick and ten inches wide. Tell them it's for Wokky. We'll need that".

'Anyway, the bobbies go and they're back in half an hour. All the blue lights flashing, an' tha', with the spare wheel, with a police car behind and this dirty, big length of timber stickin' out the window, with a bobby in the passenger seat holdin' on to it. I got the chauffeur te get the toolbox out of the Rolls Royce and place it on the ground by the back bumper. The Queen was kneelin' on the back seat, lookin' out the back window, and she shouted through the glass te me.

"'Wokky", she said. "I'm just curious. What is it you're going to do?"

'I told her majesty that her Rolls Royce was armoured and weighed over two tons. There was no jack in the car, and the police car jacks couldn't possibly lift it. So, I'd use a little trick I learnt down the docks. I slid the piece of timber over the toolbox and under the car and just walked up the plank. As I got further up the plank, the Rolls Royce lifted further and further off the ground, and I stayed there 'til they changed the wheel. Well, all the bobbies were clappin', an' the crowd were wavin' their little union jacks.

'The Queen was delighted, and she said, "Wokky, we're very grateful to you. Is there anything I can do for you?"

'I asked her Majesty if I could put me bike in the boot and could she give me a lift te the "International". I said did she think the driver knew his way. The driver turned round and just looked at me. He 'ad a great big boozer's nose. Nothin' else needed te be said. Anyway, she told the Duke to sit in the front with the driver and I got a lift te the ale 'ouse with a police escort. I said te the Queen, "D'ye fancy a bevy, Queen?"

'Ye know. Would she care te come in for a gin and tonic like. She thanked me but told me she was pushed for time and she didn't drink when she was on duty anyway'.

Finally, Wokky said that he was responsible for introducing raw boiled ham into England.

List of Dockers' Nicknames

Horse Shoe Ned: he walked around on his tiptoes.

The Angry Cat: He had white side whiskers, a hump on his back, and he walked with a slight stoop and his back arched.

Tommy Sad Tales: His wife had died and he had to look after his kids on his own.

Fill the Cot: He had a load of kids

The Diesel Fitter: He stole a pair of shoes for his wife and said, 'I wonder if these'll fit her'.

The Wonder Boy: He'd always say 'I wonder what's in tha' case'.

The Jelly: He reckoned he only needed one night of overtime and he'd be set.

The Lonely Baker: He'd say 'there's only me and me tart left now;' the kids had all left home.

Bo Bo's, later on, Bo Peep: He was always asleep, and was caught peeping through people's windows.

Vanishing Cream: He would always vanish from a job.

Francis Chitchester: He was always in the Atlantic Pub.

The Kirkby Coward: He had a cigarette burn in the back of his army overcoat that looked like a bullet hole.

The Frozen Sailor: He always wore a polo neck sweater.

Cowboy Galvin: He always wore a cowboy type hat.

The Hollywood Docker: He wore really smart clothes for the dock.

The Flight: His lad was in the RAF.

The Windy Pilot: He was always saying he was bailing out of the docks.

The Windy Kitten: He was always shouting, 'Is meow ald fella there?'

The Hen: He looked like a hen with a hooked nose.

The Nanny Goat: He had a goatee beard.

The Lemon Drop Kid: He looked like the character from a kid's film.

Little Boy Blue: He always wore blue denim jeans, jacket, and cap.

Abraham Lincoln: He always stood like Abraham Lincoln, in a statesman's manner, with a velvet collar on his Teddy boy coat.

Cinderella: He was always going home before twelve o'clock.

The Lenient Judge: He once said on a job, 'Let that guy go'.

The Piano: He complained that everyone played on him.

Frank Ifield: He once said, 'I'll remember you', (a sixties hit record).

Carrot: He had red hair.

Gitten's Kittens: Men who worked for Gerry Gitten's.

Smith's Crisps: Men who worked for Smith's.

China Skins: Men who worked at the China Berth.

The Seaforth Highlanders: A gang of men who lived in Seaforth near the docks.

Hughie Green: A docker who ran down the quay, shouting after Hughie Green.

Apple Sammy: He stole a load of apples from the dock.

Louie The Lip: He had a thick lip that looked like a roll of lino.

The Black Prince: He said he was connected to royalty.

Single Bert Hump a Chink: He wasn't married, his name was Bert, and he put a Chinese girl in the family way. (Engle Bert Humperdink).

Max Factor: He told lies and was always making things up.

The Broken Bulb: He was always broke and never had a light.

The Baldy Rabbit: He'd get on the bus with no money and say, 'I've got no fare'.

The Unknown Soldier: He always wore a khaki army jacket, was very quiet, and never spoke to anyone; nobody knew his name.

Bald Eagle: He had a bald head, a hooked nose, and looked just like an eagle.

Sinatra: He fancied himself as a crooner and always sang Sinatra songs.

The Sick Pigeon: He was always in the loft. (The upper floor of a dock shed).

Sayings and Expressions

A Glasgow Face: A neatly stowed wall of cartons, where the cartons behind have been dumped in and not stowed properly.

AP (Attendance proved): Stamped into a docker's book at the control (the pen) when there was no work. Fall back pay was paid for that morning or afternoon. Having an AP stamped was called 'signing on'.

Blowing for Tugs: Needing assistance.

Boiling Piece: Used to describe a fat, ugly woman.

Carried Away: Broken.

Cheap Jack: He sold any old shite at the gate.

Day-old Chicks: Young men just starting to work on the docks.

Down the Line: Berths not in your particular area.

Glassback: Anybody who complained about lifting.

He's a Dog's Arse or He's a Warm Order: Used to describe fellas that dockers disliked.

k-legged: Drunk and standing with legs like a letter K.

Kecks: Trousers.

Knock Off Gear: To steal or describe stolen goods.

Loading Off: Trucking cargo, cotton, or rubber, usually to the 'putter out', to lower down to lorries in the avenue at the back of the shed.

Lobo: Meaning: A culmination of some event.

A *Long Lobby*: Extra hours worked on a Sunday day shift, normally so that the work was finished and a ship could catch the tide.

A *Nugget*: A night shift of eight hours, from eleven P.M. Saturday night until seven A.M. Sunday morning, resulting in nearly a whole week's normal pay.

Paddy Kelly: A cry that meant a policeman was coming along the dock.

Sling Your Hook: To tell someone to get lost.

Take a Powder: Meaning, 'get lost', or 'go away'.

Talking Spanish: When somebody is drunk and can't be understood.

The Atlantic Roll: Seafarer's walk.

The Clearing House: Where dockers went to pick their wages up.

Three Sheets to the Wind: Very confused.

Working for the Queen: When a docker signed on
all week practically, and was given a job
right at the end when it made no difference
to the fall back pay received.

You Can't Work in Convulsions: Spoken to
someone who was lazy.

Your Bars Are Down: When a stupid decision has
been made.

Names for Dock Equipment

A goods wire: A thin steel cable.

A leg: A cable threaded through a smaller hook,
doubled, and with both eyes hooked on
to the large hook of the crane, making it
easier to handle.

A sling: A Continuous loop of rope.

A Snotter: A single rope with an eye in each end.

A Sweep: Normally twenty feet long, a half-inch-
thick cable for heavier lifting.

Dunnage: Pieces of wood of all sizes and
thicknesses used to make sure the cargo
on a ship is more or less level.

The Fall: The cable that came down the hatch to
hook slings on to.

Nautical Names

Deck: The floor.

Bulkhead: The wall.

Deckhead: The ceiling.

The Combings: What you can't see looking down the hatch of a ship. The extra room underneath and away from the square.

The Square of the Hatch: What you can see down from the deck.

Some Pubs Frequented by Dockers

The Caradoc; The Royal; The International; The Winnies; The Castle and The Langton.

Seven Miles of Liverpool Docks

North Liverpool Docks Opening Dates

Seaforth 1972

Gladstone 1927

Gladstone Graving 1913

Hornby 1884

Alexandra 1881

Langton 1881

Brocklebank 1862

Canada 1859

Huskisson 1852

Sandon 1851

Wellington 1850

Bramley-Moore 1848

Nelson 1848

Salisbury 1848

Collingwood 1848

Stanley 1848

Trafalgar 1836

Waterloo 1834

Princes 1810

South Liverpool Docks Opening Dates

Canning 1737

Old Dock 1709

Salthouse 1753

Albert 1841

Dukes 1773

Kings 1785

Wapping 1852

Queens 1785

Coburg 1840

Brunswick 1832

Toxteth 1841

Harrington 1882

Herculaneum 1866

If you would like to contact the authors of this book: Tony and Lorraine Sanders, their email address is: www.blush@hotmail.com

Made in the USA
Lexington, KY
26 November 2009